DATE DUE

INTRODUCING
ISSUES WITH
OPPOSING
VIEWPOINTS®

Fast Food

Lauri S. Scherer, *Book Editor*

GREENHAVEN PRESS
A part of Gale, Cengage Learning

GALE
CENGAGE Learning·

Detroit • New York • San Francisco • New Haven, Conn • Waterville, Maine • London

Elizabeth Des Chenes, Director, Content Strategy
Cynthia Sanner, Publisher
Douglas Dentino, Manager, New Product

Articles in Greenhaven Press anthologies are often edited for length to meet page requirements. In addition, original titles of these works are changed to clearly present the main thesis and to explicitly indicate the author's opinion. Every effort is made to ensure that Greenhaven Press accurately reflects the original intent of the authors. Every effort has been made to trace the owners of copyrighted material.

Cover image © Ministr-84/Shutterstock.com.

LIBRARY OF CONGRESS CATALOGING-IN-PUBLICATION DATA

Fast food / Lauri S. Scherer, book editor.
    pages cm. -- (Introducing issues with opposing viewpoints)
  Audience: Age 14 to 18.
  Includes bibliographical references and index.
  ISBN 978-0-7377-6922-7
  1. Convenience foods--United States--Juvenile literature. 2. Convenience foods--Health aspects--United States--Juvenile literature. 3. Fast food restaurants--United States--Juvenile literature. I. Scherer, Lauri S.
  TX370.F365 2013
  642'.1--dc23

                                    2013002536

Printed in the United States of America
1 2 3 4 5 6 7 16 15 14 13 12

Contents

Chapter 3: Should Restrictions Be Placed on Fast Food?

Foreword

Indulging in a wide spectrum of ideas, beliefs, and perspectives is a critical cornerstone of democracy. After all, it is often debates over differences of opinion, such as whether to legalize abortion, how to treat prisoners, or when to enact the death penalty, that shape our society and drive it forward. Such diversity of thought is frequently regarded as the hallmark of a healthy and civilized culture. As the Reverend Clifford Schutjer of the First Congregational Church in Mansfield, Ohio, declared in a 2001 sermon, "Surrounding oneself with only like-minded people, restricting what we listen to or read only to what we find agreeable is irresponsible. Refusing to entertain doubts once we make up our minds is a subtle but deadly form of arrogance." With this advice in mind, Introducing Issues with Opposing Viewpoints books aim to open readers' minds to the critically divergent views that comprise our world's most important debates.

Introducing Issues with Opposing Viewpoints simplifies for students the enormous and often overwhelming mass of material now available via print and electronic media. Collected in every volume is an array of opinions that captures the essence of a particular controversy or topic. Introducing Issues with Opposing Viewpoints books embody the spirit of nineteenth-century journalist Charles A. Dana's axiom: "Fight for your opinions, but do not believe that they contain the whole truth, or the only truth." Absorbing such contrasting opinions teaches students to analyze the strength of an argument and compare it to its opposition. From this process readers can inform and strengthen their own opinions, or be exposed to new information that will change their minds. Introducing Issues with Opposing Viewpoints is a mosaic of different voices. The authors are statesmen, pundits, academics, journalists, corporations, and ordinary people who have felt compelled to share their experiences and ideas in a public forum. Their words have been collected from newspapers, journals, books, speeches, interviews, and the Internet, the fastest growing body of opinionated material in the world.

Introducing Issues with Opposing Viewpoints shares many of the well-known features of its critically acclaimed parent series, Opposing Viewpoints. The articles are presented in a pro/con format, allowing readers to absorb divergent perspectives side by side. Active reading questions preface each viewpoint, requiring the student to approach the material thoughtfully and carefully. Useful charts, graphs, and cartoons supplement each article. A thorough introduction provides readers with crucial background on an issue. An annotated bibliography points the reader toward articles, books, and websites that contain additional information on the topic. An appendix of organizations to contact contains a wide variety of charities, nonprofit organizations, political groups, and private enterprises that each hold a position on the issue at hand. Finally, a comprehensive index allows readers to locate content quickly and efficiently.

Introducing Issues with Opposing Viewpoints is also significantly different from Opposing Viewpoints. As the series title implies, its presentation will help introduce students to the concept of opposing viewpoints and learn to use this material to aid in critical writing and debate. The series' four-color, accessible format makes the books attractive and inviting to readers of all levels. In addition, each viewpoint has been carefully edited to maximize a reader's understanding of the content. Short but thorough viewpoints capture the essence of an argument. A substantial, thought-provoking essay question placed at the end of each viewpoint asks the student to further investigate the issues raised in the viewpoint, compare and contrast two authors' arguments, or consider how one might go about forming an opinion on the topic at hand. Each viewpoint contains sidebars that include at-a-glance information and handy statistics. A Facts About section located in the back of the book further supplies students with relevant facts and figures.

Following in the tradition of the Opposing Viewpoints series, Greenhaven Press continues to provide readers with invaluable exposure to the controversial issues that shape our world. As John Stuart Mill once wrote: "The only way in which a human being can make some approach to knowing the whole of a subject is by hearing what can be said about it by persons of every variety of opinion and studying all modes in which it can be looked at by every character of mind. No wise man ever acquired his wisdom in any mode but this." It is to this principle that Introducing Issues with Opposing Viewpoints books are dedicated.

Introduction

America is known for its love of fast food and, increasingly, for fast-food experiences that embrace extreme eating and "challenge" dishes. In Pittsburgh, for example, Denny's Beer Barrel Pub serves a six-pound hamburger, while the nearby Jerome Bettis' Grille offers a 36-ounce steak. Jack-n-Grill, located in Denver, Colorado, serves a seven-pound burrito filled with a dozen eggs, a half pound of cheese, and a half pound of ham. This extreme breakfast is modest compared to what is offered by the Broken Yolk, a California brunch restaurant's twelve-egg omelet served on a fifteen-inch pizza tray, stuffed with a half pound of cheese and topped with chili, home fries, and two oversized biscuits. The extreme concoctions served up by these and thousands of other fast-food restaurants amplify the debate over whether people have the freedom to eat how and what they want, or whether society has the responsibility to discourage foods and portions that are known to be hazardous to health.

Perhaps the most famous extreme fast-food restaurant is the Heart Attack Grill in Las Vegas, Nevada. Famous for celebrating excess and indulgence, everything about it dares people to eat gluttonous versions of foods that are known to be bad for their health. It specializes in extremely large burgers and fries, such as the Quadruple Bypass Burger (four burger patties with bacon that consists of two pounds of meat and has eight thousand calories), Flatliner Fries (which have been deep-fried in lard), and shakes made with butterfat. These items are served up by waitresses who wear nurse uniforms, and the restaurant offers free and unlimited meals to customers who weigh more than 350 pounds.

Menu items are promoted as an over-the-top, daredevil indulgence that mimics the essence of extreme sports, in which people take known risks and delight in doing so. Jon Basso, the Heart Attack Grill's owner, puts his restaurant's offerings in these terms. "It's a lifestyle issue," Basso said of eating unhealthily. "We attract the avant-garde of lifestyle seekers."[1]

But some are wary of the Heart Attack Grill's tongue-in-cheek take on what for millions of Americans is a serious problem: obesity and its accompanying health risks. In April 2012 a woman fell unconscious at the Heart Attack Grill while eating a Double Bypass Burger, drinking a margarita, and smoking a cigarette. Just two months earlier, a customer had a heart attack while consuming the Triple Bypass Burger. Though both survived, the restaurant's 575-pound spokesperson, Blair River, died in 2011 at just twenty-nine years old; the cause of death was pneumonia, which was likely complicated by his obesity.

With these people in mind, health practitioners are offended and outraged that the restaurant makes light of the serious health risks brought on by such eating habits. "Bypass surgery is no joke to anyone who has lost a loved one to heart disease," said physician Neal Barnard of the February 2012 incident in which a man was wheeled out of the Heart Attack Grill after suffering a heart attack during his meal. "This latest emergency should be a wake-up call for the Heart Attack Grill. The restaurant should end its bizarre attempts to capitalize on obesity and clogged arteries."[2] Susan Levin, a registered dietitian, agrees. She thinks extreme eateries have a moral obligation to avoid preying on Americans' already troubled relationship with fast food: "It's time to stop profiting from human misery."[3]

In addition to restaurant chains, state fairs are a hotbed of fast foods that are not only unhealthy, but also specifically celebrated for being so. "Standard fare at these events has never been considered healthy, but fair vendors go out of their way to create increasingly ridiculous gut-busting offerings and fry up things previously thought un-fry-able,"[4] note writers at the *Huffington Post*. A sampling of foods offered at the San Diego County Fair offers but one example. Each year, this fair, held in the upscale coastal community of Del Mar, California, draws more than 1.4 million people, who come to enjoy rides, games, exhibits, and shows. Many also come to indulge in the deep-fried, fatty, salty extreme menu items intended to top the previous year's offerings.

For example, at the 2012 fair, vendors sold tens of thousands of deep-fried hot dogs, deep-fried peanut butter and jelly sandwiches, deep-fried butter balls, deep-fried Kool-Aid balls, deep-fried cereal balls, deep-fried Twinkies, deep-fried Snickers bars, deep-fried peanut butter cups, deep-fried Spam, deep-fried Tang balls, and deep-fried pickles. Customers consumed 60,000 deep-fried Oreo cookies, 180,000 deep-fried hamburgers (called "Belly Buster Burgers"), 20,000 deep-fried pineapple rings, and 1,200 deep-fried green bean orders.

A local newspaper estimated that fair visitors consumed more than 250,000 pieces of bacon, including thousands of pieces of chocolate-covered bacon.

Among the most popular items was a sandwich called the Krispy Kreme Chicken Sandwich, which featured a piece of fried chicken in between two deep-fried donuts, rather than a bun. Also popular was the Deep-Fried Chili Asteroid, an enormous serving of chili and cheese deep-fried in hush puppy batter. Topping the list of unbelievable dishes, however, may have been the Meat-on-Meat Dog—a quarter-pound beef hot dog wrapped in a quarter pound of bacon and the Caveman Turkey Club—an extra-large turkey leg wrapped in an entire pound of bacon.

Most viewed the excessive creations as an acceptable once-a-year indulgence that was separate from the nation's obesity problem. This attitude was clear in the largely positive press coverage the fair's fast foods received. Despite Southern California's reputation as one of the healthiest, most active, and most weight-conscious regions of the country, there was almost nothing critical said about the fair's gluttonous concoctions. "Batter Up!"[5] proclaimed a headline in one local paper. "Gloriously Unhealthy Fair Foods,"[6] reported the local NBC news affiliate. "These dishes may be grotesque, but we've got to give credit for ingenuity,"[7] was the take of another media outlet. "If it's deep fried, people will buy it,"[8] cheered another.

Yet others argue that celebrating excessive amounts of fat, calories, sugar, and salt in any context is emblematic of the larger problem facing Americans: Their worship of unhealthy food. Dietitian Levin argues that glorifying health-threatening products is never acceptable or condonable. "I have watched with disgust and alarm as American restaurants have raced to create over-the-top 'challenge' foods: large portions of extremely high-calorie, meat-heavy foods served up with a hefty side of contempt for the customer's health," says Levin. "It reminds me of a time when the tobacco industry glamorized cigarettes as icons of self-expression and rebellion."[9]

Whether and how the phenomenon of extreme eating contributes to the obesity problem is but one topic covered in *Introducing Issues with Opposing Viewpoints: Fast Food*. Readers will also consider whether fast food should be treated like tobacco or alcohol, whether it can be healthy, and whether regulations should be placed on its advertising.

Pro/con selections expose readers to the basic debates surrounding fast food and encourage them to develop their own opinions on the topic.

Notes

1. Quoted in Eric Pfeiffer, "Another 'Heart Attack Grill' Customer Collapses While Eating 'Bypass Burger," Yahoo! News, April 24, 2012. http://news.yahoo.com/blogs/sideshow/another-heart -attack-grill-customer-collapses-while-eating-191647836.html.
2. Quoted in Physicians Committee for Responsible Medicine, "'Shut It Down,' Doctors Tell Heart Attack Grill," February 16, 2012. www.pcrm.org/media/news/shut-it-down-doctors-tell-heart -attack-grill.
3. Susan Levin, "Extreme Eateries Prey on America's Troubled Relationship to Food," Physicians Committee for Responsible Medicine, March 14, 2012. http://pcrm.org/media/commentary /extreme-eateries-prey-on-americas-troubled.
4. *Huffington Post*, "State Fair Foods: The Most Ridiculous Concoctions of All Time," August 24, 2012. www.huffington post.com/2012/08/24/state-fair-foods-craziest_n_1827692 .html#slide=1416714.
5. Ruth Marvin Webster, "Batter Up! Fairgoers Explore Deep-Fried Wonders," *San Diego North County Times*, June 10, 2012. www .nctimes.com/news/local/del-mar/del-mar-batter-up-fairgoers -explore-deep-fried-wonders/article 30ddf50f-03ef-569c-9352 -636a9b3550a3.html.
6. NBC7 San Diego, "Gloriously Unhealthy Fair Foods," 2012. www .nbcsandiego.com/the-scene/food-drink/Gloriously-Unhealthy -Fair-Foods--94278454.html.
7. *Huffington Post*, "State Fair Foods."
8. Jonathan Horn, "How Much Deep-Fried Food Was Sold at Fair?" *San Diego Union-Tribune*, June 21, 2011. www.utsandiego.com /news/2011/iul/07/all-facts-county-fairs-fare.
9. Levin, "Extreme Eateries Prey on America's Troubled Relationship to Food."

Chapter 1

Is Fast Food Harmful?

The debate over fast food revolves around what constitutes healthy eating choices and whether fast food is making children obese.

Viewpoint

1

Fast Food Is Addictive

Kelly Brownell and Mark Gold

In the following viewpoint Kelly Brownell and Mark Gold suggest that fast food, and particularly sweets, is addictive. Comparing ingredients in these products to tobacco and alcohol, they present research showing that sugar affects the brain like a drug. It causes people to overwhelmingly desire it, set aside judgment and personal responsibility to obtain it, and stop at nothing to give their body the "fix" it craves. Such findings have enormous consequences for the fast-food industry, they say. The government—which they say has an obligation to warn people about addictive substances—should take steps to put warning labels on fast food and junk food and not allow manufacturers to sell products with ingredients that may be addictive or otherwise dangerous. They urge people to view fast food and junk food as addictive and dangerous substances on par with tobacco, alcohol, cocaine, heroin, and other addictive substances that are subject to close scrutiny.

Brownell is an expert on obesity with the Yale Rudd Center for Food Policy and Obesity. Gold is an expert on addiction with the Center for Addiction Research & Education at the University of Florida.

> *"Just like drugs of abuse, brain-rewarding effects or reinforcement from food products can lead to loss of control."*

Kelly Brownell and Mark Gold, "Food Products. Addiction. Also in the Mind," *World Nutrition*, vol. 3, no. 9, September 2012, pp. 392–405. Copyright © 2012 by Kelly Brownell. All rights reserved. Reproduced by permission.

AS YOU READ, CONSIDER THE FOLLOWING QUESTIONS:
1. What terms used to describe food do the authors say indicate addiction?
2. What did researchers Bart Hoebel and Nicole Avena discover about rats' reaction to glucose (sugar)?
3. What, according to the authors, has shifted the primal desire for calories from survivalist to destructive?

I s food and addiction a viable concept? We are sure that it is. . . . Some types of food product can act on the brain as an addictive substance. Certain constituents of food products, added sugar in particular, may hijack the brain and override human will, judgement and personal responsibility, and in so doing create a public health menace. The products most likely to trigger an addictive process appear to be those marketed most aggressively by the food manufacturing industry, which formulates and manipulates its products to maximise palatability. Just like drugs of abuse, brain-rewarding effects or reinforcement from food products can lead to loss of control. . . .

Food Is Discussed in the Language of Addiction

If we listen to what people actually say, the addiction concept seems plausible. It is common for people to use addiction-like terms to describe aspects of the ways they eat and drink. Cravings for specific food products are often described. People speak of withdrawal when they stop using products containing caffeine and added sugar. There is clear evidence that eating can map on to the diagnostic criteria for substance abuse—as an obvious example, consumption of food beyond the point where harm occurs. It is informative to examine such observations and then to see if these are supported by available science.

Food manufacturers themselves use colloquial addiction terms. They commonly advertise products as satisfying cravings, and may even refer to concepts like 'chocoholism'. Recent examples are an advertising campaign run by Dunkin Donuts for its products using the line 'Craving, Meet Your Maker', and a McDonald's campaign for the Angus Third Pounder Deluxe which said 'Crafted For Your

Craving'. This may be no more than marketing ingenuity, but it would be extremely interesting to obtain and inspect internal industry documents, to see how often the language of addiction is used in consideration of product formulation and of advertising and marketing. . . .

How Addiction Works

It is now understood that drugs of abuse hijack the brain, and that addiction is a disease of the brain. One of us (Mark Gold) has with colleagues since the 1970s worked on heroin and the *locus coeruleus* [a region of the brain that processes sensory signals], and cocaine and dopamine, and on addictions in general. During this work, it became clear that drugs of abuse cause changes in eating and weight, and that withdrawal causes opposite changes. Comparably, food is compulsively appealing to a person in early withdrawal.

While we first posited the food addiction hypothesis, we had few data. Clinical results from pre-bariatric surgery cases confirmed that drugs and alcohol interfered with appetite, and that withdrawal caused increased appetite, compulsive eating, and weight gain. Bart Hoebel and Nicole Avena showed that animals will avidly self-administer glucose, and that naloxone administration caused opiate withdrawal-like symptoms in these glucose-bingeing rats. So for these animals self-administration indicates that glucose is a drug and addiction is possible. Also, withdrawal is provoked by opiate blockade. It was a remarkable series of studies by this Princeton group, demonstrating self-administration, withdrawal, bingeing, and cross-tolerance to other drugs of abuse.

Major advances followed Nora Volkow's and Brookhaven National Laboratory's building of a positron emission tomography (PET) facility capable of scanning obese and morbidly obese patients. First, they showed that these people had down-regulation of the D2 dopamine

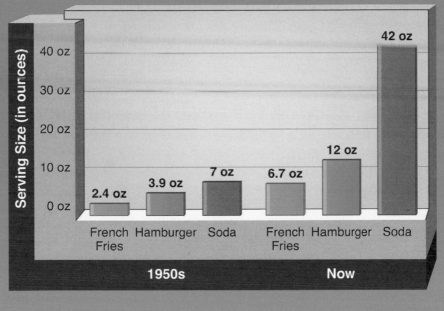

Bigger Portions, Bigger Waists

The average fast-food meal is more than four times larger than it was in the 1950s—French fry portions, hamburger servings, and soda servings have all become supersized. At the same time, the average American is 26 pounds heavier.

Taken from: Centers for Disease Control and Prevention and *The Washington Post*, May 24, 2012.

receptor, as do alcoholics and other addicts. They also showed brain-stomach connections, as well as changes in the somatosensory cortex in obesity and after bariatric surgery. The work of Gene-Jack Wang and Nora Volkow led to the conclusion that overeating and obesity changed the brain, as if practically any food consumed was a drug.

Sugar Is Like a Drug

Which substances in food are most likely to be addictive, and why? Thus far research has focused primarily on added sugar. This is justified based on biological plausibility, and also because added sugar is an important reason why calories are over-consumed. Intake of added sugar in US adolescents, for instance, is two to three times higher than recommended. The evidence suggests that such added sugar acts on the brain in ways similar to substances of abuse, strengthening the case for making foods high in added sugar a high priority for public policy.

Indeed, added sugar is already targeted as a policy priority. A great many organisations have called for reductions in sugar or sugared drink consumption, including the American Heart Association, the American Medical Association, the American Academy of Pediatrics, and the World Health Organization. Cities including New York, Los Angeles, Boston, Seattle, Philadelphia, and Cleveland have launched aggressive anti-sugared soft drink campaigns or have moved to ban the sales of such drinks in municipal facilities.

We Do Not Know the Full Extent of Ingredients' Harm

We believe that emphasis on added sugar is justified, but food products contain much more than sugar. Added fat, because it is so highly palatable and energy-dense, would be a logical constituent to examine, but has been the focus of relatively little work thus far. Individuals who direct food addiction programmes mention refined flour as a problem, but again, relatively little research has been done on this.

Processed foods contain a great many ingredients with entirely unknown effects on the brain. For example, here below is the ingredient list for a popular line, a 'Frosted Chocolate Fudge Pop Tart', which shows a stunning array of chemicals involved in the manufacture of such products:

Enriched flour (wheat flour, niacin, reduced iron, thiamine mononitrate, riboflavin, folic acid), sugar, dextrose, soybean and palm oil (with TBHQ for freshness), corn syrup, whey, cracker meal, high fructose corn syrup; contains 2 per cent or less of cornstarch, cocoa, cocoa (processed with alkali), salt, calcium carbonate, modified corn starch, leavening (baking soda, sodium acid pyrophosphate, monocalcium phosphate), mono- and diglycerides, sodium stearoyl lactylate, gelatine, egg whites, datem, xanthan gum, partially hydrogenated soybean oil, caramel color, soy lethicin, color added, vanilla extract, vitamin A palmitate, niacimide, tricalcium phosphate, reduced iron, pyridoxine hydrochloride, riboflavin, thiamine hydrochloride, folic acid.

Industry's aim is to maximise sales by enhancing the reinforcing properties of its products. A great many colourings, preservatives, fra-

Sugar, a principal ingredient in many fast foods, may hijack the brain and override human will, judgment, and personal responsibility.

grances, and 'flavour enhancers' (including caffeine, said by industry to enhance flavour) are added to food products. Manufacturers are not required to test their products for addictive effects on the brain or on the extent to which constituents of its products provoke overeating. The US Food and Drug Administration requires that food additives be GRAS (Generally Regarded As Safe), but addictive effects on the brain have not been considered relevant to considerations of safety. We think this may change.

A Primal Lust for Calories

There could well be reasons related to human evolution to explain why some foods or food products are addictive. With food needed to survive, the foods with greatest survival value, which is to say those that are most energy-dense, are the most desirable and would be consumed in large amounts when the environment provided them. Because such foods would be abundant only occasionally, mechanisms to protect against overuse would not be necessary, and eating beyond the satisfaction of short-term hunger would be adaptive, in order to maximise energy stores.

Innate drives to consume energy-dense foods are now no longer adaptive but destructive. Industrial processing by manufacturers has created products that do not appear in nature and that are stripped of constituents that slow their reinforcing properties. Much as the only mildly reinforcing coca leaves are processed into highly and immediately reinforcing cocaine, foods are made to be as immediately reinforcing as possible, creating a biological drive for more, followed by withdrawal, and so on and on, and chaos with the body's ability to regulate eating and weight. . . .

The Government Must Deal with Addictive Substances

What is to be done? Government certainly has a duty to regulate access to and the price and marketing of products known to have addictive properties. There are strict rules and regulations about sales of legal but addictive products. Their taxes are high, there are restrictions on marketing, and government compels disclosure, such that manufacturers are required by law to make declarations contrary to their commercial interest, like adding warning labels to packages.

It might now seem far-fetched to think of warning labels on some food products, or restrictions on sales of these products to minors, but such policies and actions once seemed far-fetched with tobacco and alcohol. The political power of the food manufacturing and allied industries might seem a daunting obstacle to policy change, but the tobacco industry was once considered invincible. There are now a substantial number of indications that the US and many other countries view policy change, in some cases directly confronting the interests of the manufacturers, as the hallmark of an obesity prevention strategy.

We believe that there will soon be common public awareness of the concept of food product addiction, and that attention to the issue by policy-makers will generate a number of new legislative and regulatory debates and then statutory measures.

EVALUATING THE AUTHOR'S ARGUMENTS:

Take a moment to consider the full implications of Kelly Brownell and Mark Gold's assessment of fast food—and particularly sugar—as a drug on par with tobacco, alcohol, or cocaine. If they are correct, and such foods are addictive, imagine a world in which certain food products are treated like dangerous addictive substances. What would packaging look like? How might grocery stores change or be reorganized? Would changes affect the legal or penal system? Describe some of the social, legal, and economic changes that might become commonplace in a world in which certain types of food are treated like drugs.

Big Mac Attack: *Super Size Me* Asks the Question Is McDonald's Unappealing— or Irresistible?

"Spurlock's reaction [of vomiting after eating a large meal at McDonald's] undermines his thesis that fast food is so irresistible that people can't help but gorge themselves on it."

Jacob Sullum

Jacob Sullum is a syndicated newspaper columnist with Creators Syndicate and a senior editor at *Reason* magazine. In the following viewpoint Sullum points out inconsistencies between the argument of Morgan Spurlock's documentary film *Super Size Me*— that junk food is addictive—and Spurlock's own reactions to his forced steady diet of McDonald's food. After Spurlock's first large meal at McDonald's for the documentary, he vomits the meal back up. He complains of sluggishness, depression, shortness of breath, impotence, chest pressure, and headaches, as well as boredom with the menu. Sullum suggests that such complaints indicate great effort is required to maintain a steady junk-food diet.

AS YOU READ, CONSIDER THE FOLLOWING QUESTIONS:

1. As stated by Sullum, how much weight did Morgan Spurlock gain in thirty days on his diet of McDonald's food?
2. According to the viewpoint, what does psychologist Jeffrey Schaler say about addiction?
3. As stated in the article, what advice did Jared Fogle, the formerly 425-pound star of Subway commercials, offer to an overweight girl after a speech?

D uring the first lunch of his month-long McDonald's binge, Morgan Spurlock is visibly uncomfortable. Eating in his car after stopping at a drive-through, he has trouble finishing his supersize fries. He complains of "a McBelly ache," "McGas," and "McSweats." Then he leans out the window and vomits on the asphalt.

Since Spurlock's documentary *Super Size Me* argues that fast food is addictive, perhaps this scene is a sly reference to the nausea people often experience the first time they inject heroin. On the face of it, however, Spurlock's reaction undermines his thesis that fast food is so irresistible that people can't help but gorge themselves on it. *Super Size Me* (in which I briefly appear) is full of such contradictions, and they're the best thing about the movie.

Spurlock's fast food feat consists of eating some 5,000 calories a day, twice what his doctor says he needs to maintain his starting weight of 185 pounds. He also avoids exercise because, he says, that's what most Americans do. I

> ## FAST FACT
>
> In a review published in *Nature* in 2012, Cambridge University researchers reported that addiction to high-fat, sugary processed foods has been demonstrated in animals but not in humans. Noting that there are important differences between the two, they suggested that further research is needed.

hope I'm not ruining the movie by revealing the upshot: Spurlock gains weight—nearly 25 pounds over 30 days. His cholesterol goes up, and so does his blood pressure. His doctor describes his liver function test results as "obscene." Spurlock complains of sluggishness, depression, shortness of breath, impotence, chest pressure, and headaches. Again, this experience does not seem so alluring that people would be clamoring to share it.

After nine days, Spurlock announces, "I'm pretty bored with their menu." When it's all over, he says with relief, "I can't believe that today I'm going to get up and not have to eat at McDonald's." Yet Spurlock also claims he was hooked on fast food during his binge, feeling happy only while eating. "I definitely went through serious withdrawal symptoms," including headaches, sweats, and shakes, he reported at the Washington, D.C., International Film Festival in May.

You could say Spurlock's experience reflects the reality of addiction: It's not something you fall into; you have to work hard at it. As the psychologist Jeffrey Schaler has observed, it takes "an iron will" to be an addict. But this understanding of addiction—as a choice, not a disease—works against Spurlock's attempt to blame fast food chains for making us fat.

Spurlock detracts from his message in other ways as well. Although he generally presents critics of McDonald's as public-spirited activists, he can't resist taking a shot at Samuel Hirsch, the lawyer who filed the first two obesity lawsuits against fast food restaurants. When Hirsch is asked his motive for getting involved in such litigation, he looks puzzled. "You mean, motive besides monetary compensation?" he says. "You want to hear a noble cause?" That's his only appearance in the film.

Spurlock also has a bit of fun with litigation enthusiast John Banzhaf, who somberly explains how fast food chains, like tobacco companies, "lure young children," teaching them to associate their brands with positive images and happy experiences. Spurlock deadpans, "That's why, when I have kids, every time I drive by a fast food restaurant, I'm going to punch my kids in the face."

Spurlock uses humor to advance his thesis too. He shows pictures of famous personalities to kids who look to be about 6. They readily identify Ronald McDonald and George Washington but are stumped by a third picture. "George W. Bush?" one little boy ventures, "No, but that's a good guess," says Spurlock, turning the picture toward the camera. It's a drawing of Jesus Christ.

As with Spurlock's exercise in extreme eating, I'm not sure what that proves. The fact that kids know who Ronald McDonald is does not mean they will end up gorging themselves, Spurlock-style, and become dangerously overweight.

Similarly, Spurlock asks a group of tourists to stand in front of the White House and recite the Pledge of Allegiance, which they have trouble doing accurately and in unison. But when he asks about the components of a Big Mac, one of them rattles off, "Two all-beef patties special sauce lettuce cheese pickles onions on a sesame seed bun." I can recite that list too, but I've never eaten a Big Mac.

Presumably these tests are meant to illustrate the "toxic food environment" that Yale obesity expert Kelly Brownell, who appears in the movie, blames for Americans' bulging bellies. Brownell's message—that we will continue getting fatter as long as food is cheap, tasty, readily available, and heavily promoted—is not exactly empowering. *Super Size Me* implicitly criticizes Jared Fogle, the formerly 425-pound star of Subway commercials, for offering impractical, simplistic weight loss tips. But what Fogle tells an overweight girl after a speech seems like good advice to me: "The world's not going to change. You have to change."

EVALUATING THE AUTHOR'S ARGUMENTS:

Jacob Sullum suggests that fast-food may be unappealing and that fast-food addicts have to work at being addicts. Do you agree with Sullum's assessment? Explain why or why not.

Eating Fast Food and Junk Food Has Serious Health Consequences

George Monbiot

"Alzheimer's disease could be another catastrophic impact of the junk food industry, and the worst discovered so far."

Millions of people around the world suffer from Alzheimer's disease, a debilitating form of dementia. In the following viewpoint George Monbiot suggests that eating too much junk food might cause Alzheimer's. He discusses how scientists are beginning to think of Alzheimer's as a metabolic disease, meaning it is linked to how the body processes sugar. Some go so far as to regard it as a new form of diabetes, which can be caused by overindulging in fatty, sweet foods and not getting enough exercise. Alzheimer's is a particularly feared disease: It robs people of their personalities and memories and makes them entirely dependent on others for care, unable to recognize loved ones. Monbiot says the public should pay careful attention to emerging research that links Alzheimer's to fast food and junk food and begin restricting their intake of such foods now, before it is too late. Monbiot is a reporter for the *Guardian*, a British newspaper.

AS YOU READ, CONSIDER THE FOLLOWING QUESTIONS:
1. What new name are some scientists giving Alzheimer's disease?
2. How many times more likely are type 2 diabetes sufferers to develop Alzheimer's disease?
3. What are the consequences of having a scarcely regulated food industry, according to Monbiot? Name at least two.

W hen you raise the subject of over-eating and obesity, you often see people at their worst. The comment threads discussing these issues reveal a legion of bullies who appear to delight in other people's problems.

Obesity Is Everyone's Problem

When alcoholism and drug addiction are discussed, the tone tends to be sympathetic. When obesity is discussed, the conversation is dominated by mockery and blame, though the evidence suggests that it may be driven by similar forms of addiction.

I suspect that much of this mockery is a coded form of snobbery: the strong association between poor diets and poverty allows people to use this issue as a cipher for something else they want to say, which is less socially acceptable.

But this problem belongs to all of us. Even if you can detach yourself from the suffering caused by diseases arising from bad diets, you will carry the cost, as a growing proportion of the health budget will be used to address them. The cost—measured in both human suffering and money—could be far greater than we imagined. A large body of evidence now suggests that Alzheimer's is primarily a metabolic disease. Some scientists have gone so far as to rename it: they call it type 3 diabetes.

A New Reason to Care

New Scientist carried this story on its cover on 1 September [2012]; since then I've been sitting in the library, trying to discover whether it stands up. I've now read dozens of papers on the subject, testing my cognitive powers to the limit as I've tried to get to grips with brain chemistry. Though the story is by no means complete, the evidence so far is compelling.

About 35 million people suffer from Alzheimer's disease worldwide; current projections, based on the rate at which the population ages, suggest that this will rise to 100 million by 2050. But if, as many scientists now believe, it is caused largely by the brain's impaired response to insulin, the numbers could rise much further. In the United States, the percentage of the population with type 2 diabetes, which is strongly linked to obesity, has almost trebled in 30 years. If Alzheimer's, or "type 3 diabetes", goes the same way, the potential for human suffering is incalculable.

The Alzheimer's-Sugar Connection

Insulin is the hormone that prompts the liver, muscles and fat to absorb sugar from the blood. Type 2 diabetes is caused by excessive blood glucose, resulting either from a deficiency of insulin produced by the pancreas, or resistance to its signals by the organs that would usually take up the glucose.

> # FAST FACT
>
> A 2012 study in the American Heart Association's journal *Circulation* discovered that adults who eat fast food at least twice a week are 27 percent more likely to develop diabetes and 56 percent more likely to die from heart disease than those who do not.

The association between Alzheimer's and type 2 diabetes is long-established: type 2 sufferers are two to three times more likely to be struck by this form of dementia than the general population. There are also associations between Alzheimer's and obesity and Alzheimer's and metabolic syndrome (a complex of diet-related pathologies).

Researchers first proposed that Alzheimer's was another form of diabetes in 2005. The authors of the original paper investigated the brains of 54 corpses, 28 of which belonged to people who had died of the disease. They found that the levels of both insulin and insulin-like growth factors in the brains of Alzheimer's patients were much lower than those in the brains of people who had died of other causes. Levels were lowest in the parts of the brain most affected by the disease.

"Heart Attack on a Bun," cartoon by John Darkow, *Columbia (MO) Daily Tribune*, August 27, 2007, www.PoliticalCartoons.com. Copyright © 2007 by John Darkow and PoliticalCartoons.com. All rights reserved. Used with permission.

Their work led them to conclude that insulin and insulin-like growth factor are produced not only in the pancreas but also in the brain. Insulin in the brain has a host of functions: as well as glucose metabolism, it helps to regulate the transmission of signals from one nerve cell to another, and affects their growth, plasticity and survival.

What You Eat Affects Your Brain

Experiments conducted since then seem to support the link between diet and dementia, and researchers have begun to propose potential mechanisms. In common with all brain chemistry, these tend to be fantastically complex, involving, among other impacts, inflammation, stress caused by oxidation, the accumulation of one kind of brain protein and the transformation of another. I would need the next six pages of this paper even to begin to explain them, and would doubtless get it wrong. . . .

Plenty of research still needs to be done. But, if the current indications are correct, Alzheimer's disease could be another catastrophic impact of the junk food industry, and the worst discovered so far. Our

A therapist works with an Alzheimer's patient. Some scientists are beginning to think that Alzheimer's is a metabolic disease that may be linked to the way the body processes sugar.

governments, as they are in the face of all our major crises, seem to be incapable of responding.

In this country [the United Kingdom], as in many others, the government's answer to the multiple disasters caused by the consumption of too much sugar and fat is to call on both companies and consumers to regulate themselves. Before he was replaced by someone even worse, the former health secretary, Andrew Lansley, handed much of the responsibility for improving the nation's diet to food and drink companies—a strategy that would work only if they volunteered to abandon much of their business.

With Dementia, Better Safe than Sorry

A scarcely regulated food industry can engineer its products—loading them with fat, salt, sugar and high-fructose corn syrup—to bypass the neurological signals that would otherwise prompt people to stop eating. It can bombard both adults and children with advertising. It can (as we discovered yesterday [September 9, 2012]) use the freedom granted to academy schools to sell the chocolate, sweets and fizzy drinks now banned from sale in maintained schools. It can kill off the only effective system (the traffic-light label) for informing people how much fat, sugar and salt their food contains. Then it can turn to the government and blame consumers for eating the products it sells. This is class war, a war against the poor fought by the executive class in government and industry.

We cannot yet state unequivocally that poor diet is a leading cause of Alzheimer's disease, though we can say that the evidence is strong and growing. But if ever there was a case for the precautionary principle, here it is. It's not as if we lose anything by eating less rubbish. Averting a possible epidemic of this devastating disease means taking on the bullies—both those who mock people for their pathology and those who spread the pathology by peddling a lethal diet.

EVALUATING THE AUTHOR'S ARGUMENTS:

In this viewpoint George Monbiot uses facts, statistics, examples, and reasoning to make his argument that fast food has serious health consequences. He does not, however, use any quotations to support his point. If you were to rewrite this article and insert quotations, what authorities might you quote from? Where would you place your quotations, and why?

Subway Restaurants Partner with American College of Cardiology

"With a large variety of better-for-you sandwich options, consumers can make more informed food choices and take more control in managing healthier behavior."

Food and Beverage Close-Up

Food and Beverage Close-Up is a brand of Close-Up Media, which is an independent digital media company in the United States that provides news and information for busy professionals. In the following viewpoint *Food and Beverage Close-Up* reports on Subway's sponsorship of the American College of Cardiology (ACC) CardioSmart National Care Initiative. Subway's sponsorship is part of its effort to promote healthy lifestyle choices. The author mentions Subway's "Fresh Fit" choices menu options that are low in fat and include fresh vegetables. The author notes that Subway hopes to enable consumers to make more informed food choices and to have more control in managing a healthy lifestyle.

1. According to the viewpoint, what is the CardioSmart National Care Initiative of the ACC?
2. According to the viewpoint, how many meal combinations under six hundred calories does Subway offer?
3. As stated in the article, what does the growing body of evidence that the CardioSmart National Care Initiative is based on suggest?

S ubway restaurants, a restaurant chain, announced its sponsorship of the American College of Cardiology (ACC) CardioSmart National Care Initiative, which promotes awareness and heart healthiness.

The sponsorship is exclusive to Subway among quick service restaurants.

As part of the relationship with the ACC, Subway restaurants will support the CardioSmart National Care Initiative, a patient-centered campaign to engage people to play an active role in their own heart health and empower them to make better lifestyle choices.

"We are pleased to add the ACC to the organizations we work with that are devoted to healthy and active living," said Tony Pace, Subway Franchisee Advertising Fund Chief Marketing Officer. "Working with organizations like the ACC and the AHA, with which we have worked for 10 years, ensures Subway will be at the forefront of discussions about health and nutritional progress."

> **FAST FACT**
>
> McDonald's customers can order a package of apple slices or fruit and walnuts as a side dish or substitute them for french fries in a kids' meal.

Subway features 8 sandwiches under 6 grams of fat among its Subway "Fresh Fit" choices. The meal choices provide low fat and low saturated fat alternatives with personalized sandwich combinations, fresh vegetables, nutritious sides of apples, yogurt, or Baked! LAY'S Potato Crisps, and a selection of low-fat milk, diet soda, bottled water or other beverage.

"The Subway menu offers at least 40 meal combinations under 600 calories and brings together nutrition and flavor that can be personalized to meet the needs and tastes of the customer," said Lanette Kovachi, M.S., R.D, corporate dietician for Subway. "With a large variety of better-for-you sandwich options, consumers can make more informed food choices and take more control in managing healthier behavior."

The CardioSmart National Care Initiative is based, in part, on the growing body of evidence suggesting that medical outcomes can be improved when people become more knowledgeable and engaged in their own health management and care. Getting early detection, prevention and disease management messages into the mainstream—where people at risk for heart disease are already engaged—has been shown to be an effective way to educate people and promote health behavior change and is also a fundamental part of successful public health interventions.

"As people become more knowledgeable about their own heart health management, wellness can improve, early detection can rise and prevention can be more successful," said Ralph Brindis, M.D., M.P.H., president of the ACC. "Making small changes in everyday choices can have a profound effect on heart health. Our partnership with organizations such as Subway help the ACC engage people through the CardioSmart National Care Initiative and empower them to live healthier lifestyles and make CardioSmart choices."

EVALUATING THE AUTHOR'S ARGUMENTS:

Food and Beverage Close-Up's report supports Subway's presentation of itself as a company concerned about the health of its customers and as a provider of healthy food. Do you agree with this presentation? Explain why or why not.

Fast Food Is Responsible for Making Children Fat

"High-fat, high-cholesterol foods like these have contributed to America's childhood obesity epidemic, which increases the risk of diabetes and other chronic diseases."

Physicians Committee for Responsible Medicine

The Physicians Committee for Responsible Medicine (PCRM) is an organization of doctors who promote preventive medicine and behaviors to improve public health. In the following viewpoint the committee argues that fast food is responsible for making kids fat. It details five popular kids' meals found at fast-food restaurants, noting that all of them exceed appropriate amounts of calories, fat, and salt for a child's single meal. Moreover, excessive consumption of these ingredients is linked to serious diseases, including heart disease, diabetes, cancer, and more. Because of their nutritional violations and their connection to debilitating, life-threatening diseases, such foods can in no way be considered part of a healthy children's diet, the committee concludes.

AS YOU READ, CONSIDER THE FOLLOWING QUESTIONS:
1. By what percentage did "healthy" fast food menu items increase between 2009 and 2010, according to the author? What problem does PCRM have with this?
2. What percentage of American children aged two to nineteen does the author say are overweight? What percentage are obese?
3. How much of a child's daily sodium intake does a McDonald's Mighty Kids Meal contain, according to the author?

As Burger King and other fast-food companies unveil new menu items marketed to children, there is growing controversy over the link between high-fat fast food and childhood obesity. One in three young people is now overweight, and children who live near fast-food restaurants are more likely to be obese, according to a recent study in the *International Journal of Pediatric Obesity*.

To determine whether heavily marketed kids meals are putting children's health at risk, dietitians with the Physicians Committee for Responsible Medicine (PCRM) analyzed menu items from five major fast-food chains.

Fast Food Is Alarmingly Bad for Kids

PCRM dietitians found that most kids meals marketed by national fast-food chains are alarmingly high in fat, cholesterol, and calories. Some contain more sodium and about as much saturated fat as a child should consume in an entire day. None of the five meals highlighted in PCRM's report meet the nutritional standards for children's meals set forward in recommendations published this year by the Institute of Medicine. . . .

It has been 30 years since McDonald's began marketing the Happy Meal to children. Since then, nearly every major fast-food restaurant has introduced a kids meal. The latest trend among these companies is promoting kids meals as healthy. A recent report found that in the last year, menu items in American fast-food chains labeled as healthy grew by 65 percent.

McDonald's Mighty Kids Meals are one example. The company says the meals are the "perfect size for those in-be-tweens." But the meal analyzed for this report has nearly double the recommended amount of fat for one meal and more than double the amount of saturated fat and sodium for one meal. Burger King says that its BK Breakfast Kids Meal "joins [the] brand's roster of meals that meet stringent nutrition criteria." But the muffin sandwich provides more than the recommended cholesterol intake for one meal.

These Foods Contribute to Child Obesity

High-fat, high-cholesterol foods like these have contributed to America's childhood obesity epidemic, which increases the risk of diabetes and other chronic diseases. Among children and adolescents ages 2 to 19 in the United States, 31.7 percent are overweight and

Many fast-food restaurants sell a "kids' meal" of some kind, which usually exceeds healthful amounts of fat, salt, and sugar and contributes to child obesity, according to the author.

16.9 percent are obese. One in three children born in the year 2000 will develop diabetes at some point in his or her life.

In August 2010, dietitians from PCRM looked at national fast-food chains' kids menus and compared nutrient content. Dietitians obtained nutrient information by reviewing the company websites and by contacting the companies directly to clarify online information.

Dietitians evaluated each item based on specific nutrition data, including the item's calories, total fat, saturated, fat, cholesterol, and sodium. Evaluations also reflect whether the product contains red or processed meats, which are linked to increased risk of colorectal cancer.

Why Fat, Salt, Cholesterol, and Calories Are a Threat

PCRM dietitians looked at several key factors to determine the healthfulness of each item:

High Fat Content: Diets high in fat have been linked by scientific research to increased risk of cancers, diabetes, and heart disease. High-fat, low-fiber foods boost the hormones that promote cancer. Specifically, diets high in meat, dairy products, fried foods, and vegetable oils cause an increase in the production of estrogen. Extra estrogen increases cancer risk in the breast and other organs sensitive to sex hormones. In January 2010, the Centers for Disease Control and Prevention found that 20 percent of adolescents ages 12 to 19 have at least one abnormal lipid level (LDL cholesterol, HDL cholesterol, or triglycerides). Among overweight and obese adolescents, those rates were higher, with 22 percent of overweight and 43 percent of obese children having one or more abnormality. Trans fats raise LDL ("bad") cholesterol levels and lower HDL ("good") cholesterol levels, increasing the risk of cardiovascular disease. Naturally occurring trans fats are only contained in animal products. Fat contains 9 calories per gram and is typically more abundant in animal products, especially saturated fat, which significantly increases bad cholesterol.

High Caloric Intake: Obesity leads to increased risk of several chronic diseases. Heart disease, diabetes, and cancer are all greatly influenced by excess weight gain. Men and women have higher levels of hormones (i.e., testosterone and estrogen) when their weight increases, making them more prone to disease. Among children and adolescents ages 2 to 19 in the United States, 31.7 percent are overweight and 16.9 percent are obese. Childhood obesity has become an epidemic in the past three decades. Among children 2 to 5 years old, obesity prevalence increased from 5 to 12.4 percent; among children 6 to 11, it increased from 6.5 to 17 percent; and among adolescents 12 to 19 years old, it increased from 5 to 17.6 percent. Maintaining a healthy weight can significantly reduce the risk of certain cancers and other life-threatening diseases.

Sodium: Diets high in sodium can increase the risk of high blood pressure, a condition that can lead to cardiovascular disease and kidney problems. The Institute of Medicine recommends that children's intake of sodium should be less than 637 to 737 milligrams (depending on age) at lunch and less than 435 to 474 milligrams (depending on age) at breakfast. Some health experts suggest consuming less than 1,500 milligrams of sodium per day.

Cholesterol: Cholesterol is a waxy substance found in the bloodstream and in the body's cells. Every animal cell contains cholesterol as it is a necessary component of the cell's membrane. The body naturally makes more than enough cholesterol to serve this biological function. High blood-cholesterol levels are strongly linked to risk of heart disease. High levels of LDL ("bad") cholesterol and low levels of HDL ("good") cholesterol increase the risk of heart disease and stroke. Saturated fats and trans fats both increase LDL levels. Consuming large amounts of cholesterol in one's diet may eventually lead to reduced heart function. Fiber helps to remove blood cholesterol and is only found in plant foods.

Red and Processed Meats: Consuming red and processed meats—including deli meats, hot dogs, hamburgers, and bacon—is a key risk factor for colorectal cancer, according to a comprehensive report released in 2007 by the American Institute for Cancer Research and the World Cancer Research Fund. There is evidence that red and processed meats are linked to other cancers as well.

The Worst of the Worst
McDonald's Mighty Kids Meal
Rating: Worst Kids Meal at a Fast-Food Restaurant

Meal items: Double cheeseburger, French fries, and chocolate milk

840 calories, 37 grams of fat, 14 grams of saturated fat, 85 milligrams of cholesterol, 1,460 milligrams of sodium

With 840 calories, 37 grams of fat, and about as much sodium as a child should consume in an entire day, the McDonald's Mighty Kids Meal tops PCRM's list of the five most unhealthful fast-food meals marketed to children. This meal contains the most calories, fat, and saturated fat of any meal analyzed.

Wendy's Kids' Meal
Rating: Second-Worst Kids Meal at a Fast-Food Restaurant

Meal items: Chicken sandwich, French fries, and chocolate Frosty

770 calories, 34 grams of fat, 9.5 grams of saturated fat, 60 milligrams of cholesterol, 1,390 milligrams of sodium

Wendy's calls this meal "kid sized." But its calories and fat are super-sized—more than one meal should contain. That's not surprising, given that it features a high-fat chicken sandwich, French fries cooked in oil, and a Frosty containing milk and cream. America's rising obesity rates reflect increased intake of oils, meat, cheese, and frozen desserts, according to a recent study published in the *American Journal of Clinical Nutrition*. Wendy's Kids' Meal contains all of these factors.

KFC Kids Meal
Rating: Third-Worst Kids Meal at a Fast-Food Restaurant

Meal Items: Popcorn chicken, potato wedges, string cheese, and soda

800 calories, 34.5 grams of fat, 7.5 grams of saturated fat, 65 milligrams of cholesterol, 1,800 mg of sodium

This meal features cholesterol-laden popcorn chicken, high-fat potato wedges, and more sodium than children 4 to 8 should consume in an entire day, according to the Institute of Medicine. The high levels of sodium commonly found in kids meals can contribute to high blood pressure and calcium loss from bones.

A&W Kids Meal

Rating: Fourth-Worst Kids Meal at a Fast-Food Restaurant

Meal Items: Cheeseburger, French fries, and soda

780 calories, 29 grams of fat, 9 grams of saturated fat, 70 milligrams of cholesterol, 1,360 milligrams of sodium

The A&W Kids Meal contains more calories, saturated fat, and sodium than the Institute of Medicine recommends for a child's lunch. High-fat, high-cholesterol foods like those found in the A&W Kids Meal are causing overweight children's arteries to resemble those of 45-year-old adults, according to a recent study. And a study published this month [August 2010] in the journal *Pediatrics* found that overweight girls show signs of puberty at a younger age, which can increase the risk of breast cancer.

BK Breakfast Kids Meal

Rating: Fifth-Worst Kids Meal at a Fast-Food Restaurant

Meal Items: Muffin sandwich, BK Fresh Apple Fries, low-fat caramel sauce, apple juice

410 calories, 11.5 grams of fat, 4 grams of saturated fat, 95 milligrams of cholesterol, 600 milligrams of sodium

This meal has more sodium than children should consume at breakfast, according to the Institute of Medicine, and it also has the most cholesterol of any item analyzed for this report. The cheese and egg push the cholesterol level well above the recommendations for one meal. The Centers for Disease Control and Prevention found that one in five teens has an abnormal cholesterol level, a risk factor for heart disease, the No. 1 cause of death in the United States.

EVALUATING THE AUTHOR'S ARGUMENTS:

To make its argument that fast food is unhealthy and contributes to childhood obesity, the Physicians Committee for Responsible Medicine breaks down the nutritional content of several different fast-food meals, highlighting their fat, salt, calories, and cholesterol, and examines the diseases to which excesses of these ingredients are connected. Did seeing a nutritional analysis of these meals influence your willingness to eat any of them? Why or why not? Explain your reasoning.

Does Fast-Food Marketing Make Kids Fat?

Baylen Linnekin

"So it's not food logos (or ads) that's the problem. Kids eat what their families feed them."

Baylen Linnekin is a lawyer and executive director of Keep Food Legal, a Washington, D.C.–based nonprofit organization that advocates in favor of food freedom. In the following viewpoint Linnekin argues that research finding obese children respond more to logos of food companies like McDonald's than to nonfood companies like BMW is unremarkable. He also says that calls for restrictions on food ads are unconstitutional. Linnekin offers research that indicates obese people are hypersensitive to food cues and suggests the responsibility for feeding children good food belongs in the home.

AS YOU READ, CONSIDER THE FOLLOWING QUESTIONS:

1. As stated by Linnekin, what is the goal of Amanda Bruce, lead researcher of the study that is the starting point for Linnekin's article?
2. According to the viewpoint, what debate is involved in a policy choice to curb food ads to reduce obesity?
3. As stated in the article, what is the source and who were the authors of the research that found that obese children are "hyper-responsive to food stimuli as compared with [healthy-weight] children"?

K ids recognize the McDonald's logo better than they do the FedEx logo. Kids are slightly more drawn to the former than to the latter. Obese kids are more drawn to the former than are healthy weight kids. These results are not patently obvious and have important policy implications.

These are some of the conclusions reached by researchers at the University of Missouri, Kansas City's B.R.A.I.N. Lab.

A new study by researchers based at the lab argues that the brains of obese youngsters are wired to respond to the logos of food companies.

"When showed images of fast food companies, the parts of the brain that control pleasure and appetite lit up," writes Makini Brice in a summary of the research at *Medical Daily*. "The brains did not do the same when showed images from companies not associated with food," including BMW and FedEx.

The authors bill their research, published in *Social Cognitive and Affective Neuroscience* (SCAN), as "the first study to examine children's brain responses to culturally familiar food and nonfood logos."

The researchers claim kids rate logos of food companies like McDonald's more "exciting" and "happier" than logos of non-food companies like BMW.

"Food logos," they conclude in SCAN, "seem to be more emotionally salient than the nonfood logos, perhaps due to the survival salience of food as a biological necessity."

While that finding seems unremarkable, and—I would argue—appears to merit a similarly routine conclusion along the lines of *Well, yes of course*, the authors see the need for policies to combat this trend.

Why?

The first clue is the research interests of the lead author, research assistant professor of psychology Amanda Bruce, Ph.D., who specializes in the "neuroimaging of obesity."

The Majority of Calories Do Not Come from Fast Food

Fast food is but one source of calories for US adults and children. The majority of calories are consumed in the home, as shown in the following charts. The author of this viewpoint contends that food choices take place primarily in the home, and thus fast food cannot be blamed for obesity.

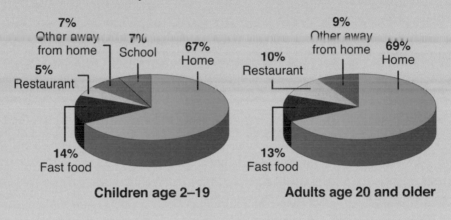

Children age 2–19

7% Other away from home
7% School
67% Home
5% Restaurant
14% Fast food

Adults age 20 and older

9% Other away from home
4% School
69% Home
10% Restaurant
13% Fast food

Taken from: USDA. Economic Research Service analysis of 2005–08 National Health and Nutrition Examination Survey data, and Joan Salge Blake. "The Healthier Side of Fast Food," Boston.com, August 28, 2012.

And, as the authors write in SCAN, "some experts have cited food marketing as one of the contributors to the recent rise in childhood obesity."

But the most obvious calls for policy changes come from Prof. Bruce herself.

"Ultimately, my down-the-road goal is to see if we can help people improve their self-control and make healthier decisions," Bruce tells the *Toronto Star*. "Because kids are limited by their underdeveloped brains, however," reports the *Star*, "that goal would mean asking: 'How moral or ethical is it to advertise to children?'"

The study's conclusions are "concerning, because the majority of foods marketed to children are unhealthy, calorifically dense foods high in sugars, fat and sodium," Bruce tells *L.A. Times* business writer David Lazarus, who took the handoff from Bruce and kept running in the same direction.

"Does that mean we should have curbs on junk-food ads, just as there are limits for cigarette and alcohol ads?" Lazarus asks. "I say yes. But I'll save the free-speech debate for another day."

While I don't find the SCAN study itself concerning—again, I think it would be stunning if the typical 12-year-old's brain showed more response to a BMW or FedEx logo than to a McDonald's logo— it's probably no surprise that I do find these policy implications inapt. And unlike Lazarus, I won't save the First Amendment implications of the policy he suggests for another day. They're unconstitutional.

Interestingly, some research that would appear to counter arguments about the particular nefariousness of food advertising and logos comes from a 2010 study by some of the same authors as the SCAN study (including lead author Bruce).

That research, published in the *International Journal of Obesity*, found that obese children are "hyper-responsive to food stimuli as compared with [healthy-weight] children." It also concludes "that many areas implicated in normal food motivation are hyper-responsive in obese groups."

In other words, obese people are probably more likely than is the average person to respond to food imagery writ large—from McDonald's logos to unbranded cheeseburger photos, and from Gogurt ads to Pinterest donut porn.

So it's not food logos (or ads) that's the problem. Kids eat what their families feed them. In spite of the arguments of Bruce, Lazarus, and others, policy change in this area should begin—and end—at home.

EVALUATING THE AUTHOR'S ARGUMENTS:

Baylen Linnekin argues that research showing that obese children are hypersensitive to food cues counters arguments about the evils of food advertising. Do you agree with Linnekin's assessment? Explain why or why not.

Fast-Food Restaurants Create "Food Deserts" in Low-Income Communities

"What does it mean for a community to lack access to adequate fresh food? Several things—and none of them good."

Jennifer Wehunt

In the following viewpoint Jennifer Wehunt discusses problems posed by "food deserts," neighborhoods that lack grocery stores but are awash in fast-food restaurants and convenience stores. Poor urban neighborhoods often lack grocery stores, which means their residents do not have easy ways to buy fruits, vegetables, meats, fish, cheese, and other healthy ingredients. Because many of these residents do not have cars, and many live in single-parent households, traveling far distances to get fresh groceries is time consuming and burdensome. It becomes much easier for such residents to turn to the abundance of nearby fast-food restaurants and convenience stores. Residents suffer as a result, Wehunt asserts: Their higher intake of fast and junk food makes them more likely to die from cancer, heart disease, and other diet-related illnesses than residents of neighborhoods in which healthy food is plentiful and easy to obtain. Wehunt is a reporter for *Chicago Magazine*.

AS YOU READ, CONSIDER THE FOLLOWING QUESTIONS:
1. How many households in Chicago's food deserts lack cars, according to Wehunt?
2. How many single mothers does the author say live within Chicago's food deserts?
3. In neighborhoods with the worst access to fresh food, how many people die of cancer? How does this compare with cancer deaths in neighborhoods with good food availability?

In the northeast corner of 101st Street and Princeton Avenue [in Chicago], a peeling sign lists activities forbidden by the 100th South Princeton Block Club: loitering, drug dealing, loud music. When Edith Howard moved from the projects to this block of brick bungalows in 1964, the neighborhood—Roseland—seemed a promising place to give her growing family a better life. But the Roseland of today is much changed: The block club hasn't been active for years, and drug and gang activity is common. What's more, Roseland lacks many of the basic resources that stabilize a neighborhood, including a good place to buy food. For groceries, Howard, 78, relies on her daughter to drive her the two and a half miles up to Chatham or down to the border of Morgan Park. "I used to shop in Roseland, but I never go over there now," Howard says of the string of sneaker shops and discount clothing stores on Michigan Avenue. "There's nothing to go there for. Everywhere I used to shop has moved away."

Life in the Food Desert

Howard is one of the 609,034 Chicagoans who live in what's known as a food desert, a concentrated area short on access to fresh meat and produce, but flush with the packaged and fried yield of convenience stores and fast-food outlets. Mari Gallagher, of Mari Gallagher Research & Consulting Group and the National Center for Public

Research, popularized the term in 2006, when she released a report on the phenomenon for LaSalle Bank. In the three years since, much has changed in the desert: The number of Chicagoans living within its boundaries has decreased, albeit slightly; at least one retailer is finding opportunity for growth in the affected areas; the green movement is taking hold, with farmers' markets and backyard gardens blooming; and leaders are recognizing that community education—on eating healthfully, on creating a demand for grocery stores—is critical. And yet, the desert remains.

What qualifies as a food desert? A cluster of blocks without a corner grocery doesn't by itself warrant the label; an entire neighborhood, or a cluster of neighborhoods, without a mainstream grocery store—such as a Jewel, a Treasure Island, or an Aldi—almost certainly does. Gallagher has identified three separate expanses within the city limits totaling 44 square miles where access to fresh and healthful food falls notably short: an elongated ring connecting the Near North Side with Lawndale and Austin; an upside-down Y stretching from the Near South Side to Ashburn and Greater Grand Crossing; and a meandering mass swallowing most of the Far South Side.

FAST FACT

A 2011 article in the *Week* reported that there are five fast-food restaurants for every grocery store in America.

Lack of Access Drives People to Fast Food

While portions of neighborhoods such as West Town fall within these boundaries, Chicago's food desert lies entirely below Division Street, affecting a population that is overwhelmingly African American: about 478,000 blacks, compared with some 78,000 whites and 57,000 Latinos, according to Gallagher's calculations. For her 2006 report, Gallagher measured the distance from the geographic center of each of the city's 18,888 inhabited blocks and found that not only do residents living in majority African American blocks travel the farthest on average to reach any type of grocery store—0.59 miles as opposed to 0.39 miles for majority-white blocks or 0.36 miles for Latinos—but they must travel twice as far to reach a grocery store as a fast-food restaurant.

What does it mean for a community to lack access to adequate fresh food? Several things—and none of them good. Day to day, residents must leave their neighborhoods for basics such as raw meat and fresh vegetables. Edith Howard, whose daughter drives her to the store, is better off than many. An estimated 64,000 households in food deserts don't have cars, so a weekly shopping trip can require cobbling together a multibus route. If the hassle of schlepping grocery bags on the CTA [Chicago Transit Authority bus and train service] sounds tiring—especially given that 109,000 food desert residents are single mothers—that's because it is. Many simply opt out, ducking into a fast-food outlet or a convenience store instead, where the inventory often runs more toward potato chips and liquor than spinach and oranges, and where a banana that would cost 29 cents at Dominick's goes for around 70 cents, if it's even available.

The Health Effects

"Diet has a direct link to obesity, diabetes, and other diseases, and you can't choose a healthy diet if you don't have access to it," Gallagher says. "Many in the food desert who suffer are children who already have diabetes but who have yet to be diagnosed and treated."

Although other factors such as poor health care and stress are likely contributors, Gallagher found that, among those living in neighborhoods with the worst access to fresh food, ten out of every 1,000 people die from cancer, as opposed to fewer than seven per 1,000 in neighborhoods with the best food availability. The comparison is even bleaker when it comes to deaths from cardiovascular disease: 11 per 1,000 in the hardest-hit neighborhoods, compared with fewer than six per 1,000 among the best off. And because nearly one-third of Chicago's food-desert residents are children, these latent repercussions have years to germinate.

The Ever-Changing Desert

Gallagher has found one small reason for hope: The desert has shrunk. When she first canvassed the city in 2006, she counted 632,974 Chicagoans living within the boundaries she established. Last fall [2008] she revisited the data, recalculating food access for each city

In many poor urban areas fast-food restaurants outnumber grocery stores.

block, taking into account every grocery store opening and closing since 2006. The result? A modest but encouraging 23,940 fewer Chicagoans living in the desert.

The decline doesn't necessarily signal a trend, however. Much like a literal desert, a food desert is an ever-shifting organism, constantly claiming a few blocks here as it cedes a few blocks there. A Food-4-Less that opened in September 2006 in West Englewood positively impacted some 307 city blocks—or 40,712 residents, 13,626 of them children—but the closing of a Dominick's and a Cub Foods in neighboring Chatham adversely affected 16,032 residents, worsening food access for 142 city blocks. (Wal-Mart has eyed Chatham as a potential area for development, but as long as the city vetoes the nonunion megastore's expansion beyond its one Chicago site, additional locations remain off the table.) In total, between summer 2006 and fall 2008, the boundaries of the city's food desert withdrew in certain areas, leaving 52,836 residents with improved food access, but elsewhere grew to encompass another 28,896 Chicagoans who previously were not classified as living within the desert.

No Single Solution

"The food desert is not one single problem with one single solution," Gallagher says, but one clear strategy, developing new stores, could have broad impact on Chicago's food access. That's why the Chicago Grocer Expo project—a group including Gallagher and city representatives—identified six priority sites, many city-owned and vacant, on the South and West sides best suited for new-store development. Unfortunately, the group released its list in September 2008, just in time for the economy's free fall. Molly Sullivan of the Chicago Department of Community Development says that while the city has held preliminary discussions with retailers regarding the targeted locations and has appointed its own task force to streamline the process for launching new stores, no lease has been signed on any of the six sites [as of July 2009].

Recession aside, opening new grocery stores is not as simple as identifying a promising site. "The food desert is only part of the story—these are business deserts," says Dr. Terry Mason, commissioner of the Chicago Department of Public Health, who recalls three nearby grocery stores—now long departed—when he was growing up in Englewood. "These neighborhoods are blighted and unsafe. There's a poor tax: Things in these neighborhoods cost more, and it's more difficult for businesses to operate there."

EVALUATING THE AUTHOR'S ARGUMENTS:

Think about your neighborhood and the places where you and your neighbors get food. Using an online map program, chart the distances from your house to the two nearest grocery stores, the two nearest fast-food restaurants, and the two nearest convenience stores. Which kinds of stores are nearest to you? Which are furthest? In what way do these stores' proximity to your house impact the kind of food you eat?

So-Called Food Deserts Do Not Really Exist

Peter Wilson

"The food desert concept overlooks the daily mobility of the American population."

In the following viewpoint Peter Wilson questions the entire premise of the "food desert," a geographic area that lacks access to healthy, fresh food and grocery stores but is awash in fast food or convenience stores that sell junk food. He takes issue with government reports that claim millions of people live prohibitively far from grocery stores. In most cases, says Wilson, "food desert" residents are just a few minutes farther from a grocery store, which he says is not prohibitive if they really want to get fresh food. Furthermore, he says, Americans are increasingly mobile—many travel ten or twenty miles to get to their job, and surely they pass many grocery stores on their way. Finally, Wilson presents evidence showing that most low-income families get food and produce from supercenters like Walmart, a circumstance that he says proves they are willing to leave their communities to get food when they want it. Wilson concludes that food deserts have been exaggerated so the federal government has an excuse to barge into small communities and tell them what is good for them. Wilson writes for the *American Thinker*, a conservative-leaning news magazine.

AS YOU READ, CONSIDER THE FOLLOWING QUESTIONS:
1. According to Wilson, how much longer does it take food desert residents than nonresidents to reach a grocery store?
2. What percentage of the US population does Wilson say lives more than a mile from a grocery store and does not have a car?
3. How much does Wilson say the government wants to spend bringing grocery stores to underserved areas?

A "food desert" is an area without a grocery store. For example, the Mojave Desert. Food deserts have been targeted by the White House, which has budgeted $400 million . . . a year for an intrusive nanny-state solution to solve a nonexistent problem.

The Government Intrudes

First Lady Michelle Obama defined the problem at the Childhood Obesity Summit at the White House on Friday [April 9, 2010], one of the four program areas of her "Let's Move" campaign:

> We can do much more to make sure that all families have access to healthy and affordable food in their own communities. Twenty-three point five million Americans, including 6.5 million children, live in communities without a supermarket. . . . So, we're working with the private sector to reach a very ambitious goal, and that is to completely eliminate food deserts in this country.

Now that the federal government is responsible for any health problems caused by the things you put in your mouth, the federal government is obliged to intervene. If you live in a food desert where the only available choice is between fast food French fries and convenience store Twinkies, you have no choice but to eat junk food, according to the First Lady.

A Strange Definition of Going Without

Consider, however, that a food desert is defined by the USDA [US Department of Agriculture] and on the Let's Move website as "neighborhoods that are more than a mile from a supermarket." Stop for a second to wrap your mind around that. If your grocery store is more than a mile away, the federal government defines your community as "without a supermarket."

When Mrs. Obama cites 23.5 million people living in food deserts, she of course doesn't include Robert Redford's ranch in Park City. She's reaching a hand out to "low-income communities." A U.S. Department of Agriculture report, "Access to Affordable and Nutritious Food: Measuring and Understanding Food Deserts and Their Consequences," cited on the Letsmove.gov site, however, makes an important distinction not mentioned by Mrs. Obama:

> Not all of these 23.5 million people have low income. If estimates are restricted to consider only low-income people in low-income areas, then 11.5 million people, or 4.1 percent of the total U.S. population, live in low-income areas more than 1 mile from a supermarket.

The report continues:

> Data on time use and travel mode show that people living in low-income areas with limited access spend significantly more time (19.5 minutes) traveling to a grocery store than the national average (15 minutes). However, 93 percent of those who live in low-income areas with limited access traveled to the grocery store in a vehicle they or another household member drove.

A Non-Problem That Affects Very Few

To summarize the USDA findings: 11.5 million people spend 4.5 minutes longer traveling to the grocery store. Does this qualify as "significantly more time"? Of this number, 7%, or 805,000 people, have to walk or take public transportation to the grocery store. Therefore the food desert problem—people more than a mile from a grocery store without a car—afflicts 0.2% of the U.S. population.

An unkind person could point out that liberals normally want to get us out of our cars, praising the health benefits of walking and the low carbon footprint of public transportation. In this case—and I agree—they believe that carrying home groceries without a car is a burden.

Myths of the "Food Desert"

A 2010 study by the University of Washington Center for Public Health Nutrition dispelled some myths of the food desert. They found that low-income shoppers *do* have ample access to grocery stores like Albertsons and Safeway and that shoppers of all income levels travel to get to food outlets. Rather than lack of access, the price of food and other habits prevented them from buying healthier items.

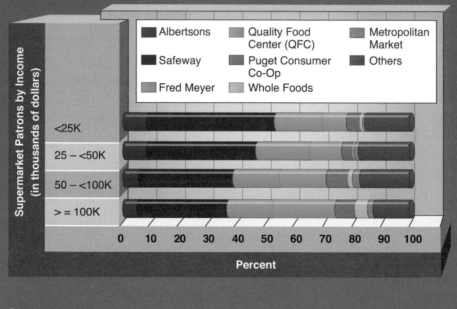

Taken from: Adam Drewnowski, Anjo Aggarwal, and Anne Vernez Moudon. *The Supermarket Gap: How to Ensure Equitable Access to Affordable Healthy Foods.* University of Washington Center for Public Health Nutrition, May 2010.

Therefore, these underprivileged people are left with only fast food and convenience stores, right? Not exactly. The USDA studied "40,000 demographically representative households across the United States." They found that convenience store "prices paid for similar goods are, on average, higher than at supermarkets." Who would have thought? More significantly:

> Food purchases at convenience stores make up a small portion of total food expenditures (2 to 3 percent) for low-income consumers. Low- and middle-income households are more likely to

purchase food at supercenters, where prices are lower.

How to address this veritable epidemic? Not to worry. Big government to the rescue! Let's Move reports:

As part of the President's proposed FY 2011 budget, the Administration announced a new program—the Healthy Food Financing Initiative—a partnership between the U.S. Departments of Treasury, Agriculture and Health and Human Services which will invest $400 million a year to provide innovative financing to bring grocery stores to underserved areas and help places such as convenience stores and bodegas carry healthier food options. Grants will also help bring farmers markets and fresh foods into underserved communities, boosting both family health and local economies. Through these initiatives and private sector engagement, the Administration will work to eliminate food deserts across the country within seven years.

We're going to "invest" $400 million a year to have federal agents "bring grocery stores to underserved areas" and "help" convenience stores carry (high-priced) apples and tomatoes? How exactly do federally funded farmers markets "boost local economies"? If the feds insisted on getting involved, wouldn't it be simpler to sign people up for a home delivery service like Peapod?

Michelle Obama, however, sees low-income people as victims incapable of taking responsibility for their family's diets. You can see the attitude in her White House speech:

[Living in a food desert] means far fewer healthier options are available to so many families who are going to be working to try to figure this out. They won't have access to the resources they need to do what we're asking them to do.

The author believes that First Lady Michelle Obama's (pictured) Let's Move! campaign against obesity is simply an attempt by the federal government to control people's choices.

It's reminiscent of her imperious speech during the campaign: "Barack Obama will require you to work. . . . Barack will never allow you to go back to your lives as usual," . . . etc. She sees government in control; families "*are going to be working*"; government is "asking" them to eat healthy food, and government then has to provide "the resources they need."

Americans Can Reach Healthy Food If They Want To

The food desert concept overlooks the daily mobility of the American population. People often commute ten or twenty miles to work, passing grocery stores along their routes. In rural communities, people who choose to live more than a mile from a grocery store typically drive into town every day for work or school. Furthermore, parents who are motivated to feed healthy food to their children won't give up because their commute to the grocery store is 4.5 minutes longer than the national average.

People are also willing to drive a lot farther than one mile to go to "supercenters, where prices are lower." Any chance that the Obama administration doesn't like people shopping at Walmart?

I don't deny that too many kids eat too much junk food. I volunteer at a charter school with a low-income population, where a typical breakfast is a candy bar on the way to school. The school's contribution is to add a nutrition class to the curriculum. Health education is important; you can build federally subsidized grocery stores to compete with Walmart, but you can't force people to buy healthy food. Not yet, anyway.

EVALUATING THE AUTHOR'S ARGUMENTS:

In this viewpoint Peter Wilson says a few extra minutes or miles will not realistically prevent anyone who really wants to go to a grocery store from getting there. Do you agree with him? Why or why not? Use evidence from the viewpoints you have read to support your argument.

Chapter 2

How Should Fast Food Be Marketed?

The way fast food is marketed is at the center of controversy around what constitutes healthy food choices.

Toys Should Only Be Included in Kids' Fast-Food Meals That Meet Nutrition Standards

Center for Science in the Public Interest

"The practice of enticing children to desire unhealthy meals using the prospect of getting a toy manipulates children's inherent trust and lack of developmental maturity."

The Center for Science in the Public Interest is a nonprofit organization that advocates for nutrition and health, food safety, alcohol policy, and sound science. In the following viewpoint the center argues that toys should be removed from unhealthy children's fast-food meals. It explains that children's brains are not yet developed enough to understand that advertising is meant to persuade them; they thus have no defenses against companies that spend millions of dollars to get them to desire their product. Including a toy in a meal preys upon children's vulnerability in a particularly insidious way, claim the authors, because it lures them toward foods that are high in calories, fat, and sodium. The author suggests that if meals are to include toys, they must meet minimum nutrition standards first.

AS YOU READ, CONSIDER THE FOLLOWING QUESTIONS:
1. How much do fast-food companies spend on giving away toys with food, according to the authors?
2. What does the author say about the comprehension ability of children under age eight?
3. According to the authors, what are some of the healthier options for children's meals that some fast-food companies promote in their advertising?

Fast-food companies target children and adolescents with $520 million worth of marketing each year, promoting products, brands, and toy premiums to kids as young as 2 years old.

- Toy giveaways make up more than half ($360 million) of that money, a marketing expenditure second only to TV advertising.
- Fast-food restaurants sell more than 1.2 billion children's meals with toys each year.
- Two-thirds of child-targeted advertising during preschool programming promotes fast-food restaurants.

Violating Children's Trust

Food and beverage marketing, including toy giveaways, influences children's food preferences, food choices, diets, and health. Preschool-aged children recognize and prefer fast food and soda brands that are extensively marketed to them. Studies show that repeated exposure to fast food and soda, through advertising, marketing, and consumption, cultivates a pattern for future consumption and a preference for those and similar foods.

Children under the age of 8 are unable to comprehend that the intent of advertising is to persuade them. The practice of enticing children to desire unhealthy meals using the prospect of getting a toy manipulates children's inherent trust and lack of developmental maturity.

The vast majority of kids' meals contain calorie-dense, nutritionally poor foods as the default. The overwhelming majority (93%) of children's meals at the nation's largest chain restaurants are high in calories; many also are high in sodium (86%) and saturated fat (45%). In a national study on default options offered with McDonald's Happy Meals, cashiers gave customers French fries 93% of the time, without even asking. Choices were usually offered for beverages, but soda was the first option offered 78% of the time. Studies of Burger King, Wendy's, and Taco Bell show similar results.

What Companies Spend on Toy Giveaways

In just one year, fast-food restaurants sold 1.2 billion meals with toys to children. Of the $520 million these corporations spent marketing their products to children, about 69 percent—or $360 million—was spent on toys. Advocates of toy bans say they unfairly lure kids to unhealthy foods.

31%
Other types
of marketing

69%
Toy giveaways
and promotions

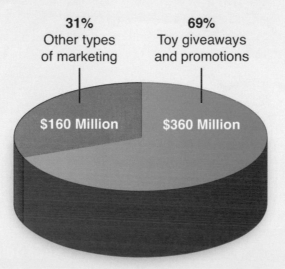

$160 Million $360 Million

Taken from: Federal Trade Commission. *Marketing Food to Children and Adolescents: A Review of Industry Expenditures, Activities, and Self-Regulation*, 2008, p. 20.

Support Parents, Protect Kids

Parents' responsibility and ability to feed their children healthfully is undermined by the marketing directed at their children and by others who also feed children and influence their food choices. Restaurants should work with parents, not against them.

Several fast-food restaurants have taken the positive step of advertising children's meals with healthier options, like apple slices, applesauce, and low-fat milk. Just as fast-food restaurants apply nutrition standards

Fast-food restaurants spend $520 million a year marketing to kids and sell 1.2 billion meals with toys each year.

to the meals they advertise, they also should apply standards to the meals they sell with toys.

Disassociating toys and other rewards from unhealthy foods is a combined responsibility that should involve states, localities, and restaurants, as well as parents. Given the sky-high rates of childhood obesity and the restaurant industry's failure to address toy giveaways with children's meals, states and localities can support parents in helping children make healthy food choices by implementing nutrition standards for children's meals that can be sold with toys.

Municipalities generally have the authority to regulate commercial products and practices to protect the public's health, safety, and general welfare. Addressing restaurant children's meals is a basic exercise of this authority.

Nutrition standards for toy giveaways with children's meals are not big government interfering with parental responsibility. Parents have the right to guide their children's food choices without so much interference from big food corporations.

EVALUATING THE AUTHOR'S ARGUMENTS:

The author of this viewpoint suggests that if toys are to be given with kids' meals at all, those meals should have to meet minimal nutritional standards. If you were to design these standards, what would they be? What kinds of foods would you recommend be included? How many calories would you recommend for such meals? How much sodium, fat, or sugar should they have? After setting your recommendations, compare those numbers and items with an actual kids' meal from a real fast-food restaurant.

Toys Should Not Be Banned from Kids' Fast-Food Meals

Michael Yaki

"*A Happy Meal toy is not a pack of Marlboros.*"

In 2011 the city of San Francisco banned fast-food restaurants from giving away free toys with children's meals. If customers want a toy, they must specifically request one and pay an additional ten cents for it (which is donated to the Ronald McDonald House of San Francisco). In the following viewpoint San Francisco attorney and resident Michael Yaki argues that this law is ridiculous. Yaki thinks it is wrong to treat toy giveaways like cigarettes or drugs. If parents are really concerned that fast food is making their children unhealthy, they can opt not to buy it for them. He also points out that kids' meals are just one way in which kids are exposed to unhealthy foods, and he says it is pointless to target fast-food restaurants when many other companies peddle unhealthy food to children. Yaki concludes that removing toys from fast-food meals is an ineffective way to combat the very real problem of childhood obesity.

AS YOU READ, CONSIDER THE FOLLOWING QUESTIONS:
1. What does the phrase "popgun approach" mean in the context of the viewpoint?
2. What does Yaki predict fast-food restaurants will eventually do to the city of San Francisco in response to the kids' meal toy ban?
3. According to Yaki, what problems plague San Francisco's children that are more serious than kids' meal toys? Name at least two.

I am going to say, flat out, that I am biased on this subject. Child obesity is no joke. The increase in diabetes is outrageous, the amount of sugar consumed by children nowadays just boggles the imagination. No right-thinking person can honestly say that million dollar advertising budgets aren't aimed at attracting kids to consume megafood conglomerates' sugary, fattening wares.

The city of San Francisco banned toys in kids' meals if the meals did not meet certain nutritional guidelines. The toys can be bought for an additional ten cents.

Toy Bans Have Little Effect on Fast-Food Restaurant Offerings

In 2010 Santa Clara, California, banned toys in fast-food children's meals that had more than 485 calories. At the time, only 4 percent of menu offerings qualified to include a toy under the new restriction. Legislators hoped the measure would encourage restaurants to provide more menu options that were under 485 calories. A year and a half later, none had.

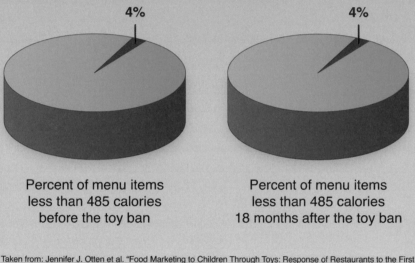

4%

4%

Percent of menu items less than 485 calories before the toy ban

Percent of menu items less than 485 calories 18 months after the toy ban

Taken from: Jennifer J. Otten et al. "Food Marketing to Children Through Toys: Response of Restaurants to the First US Toy Ordinance." *American Journal of Preventative Medicine*, vol. 42, no. 1, pp. 56–60, January 2012.

I know, better than most, how the San Francisco City Attorney works—it's the last refuge of social reformers with law degrees (which is not necessarily always a bad thing)—and some bright young attorney said that because the federal government can ban how cigarette companies behave, we can do the same thing in San Francisco with fast food chains. And, to be honest, San Francisco was one of the leading cities to go after Big Tobacco in the courts and in legislation. I supported our lawsuit against Big Tobacco on the health-related costs created by tobacco's predations. When I was on the San Francisco Employees Retirement Fund board, I successfully pushed for Fund divestment from tobacco stocks.

But a Happy Meal toy is not a pack of Marlboros.

Toys Are Not Tickets to Obesity

Banning toys in Happy Meals and requiring a "half cup of fruit" is not the same as the FCC [Federal Communications Commission] banning cigarette advertising on television, or the new restrictions on advertising, packaging, and sponsorship that the Family Smoking Prevention and Tobacco Control Act requires, which was passed by a bipartisan vote of Congress and signed into law by President [Barack] Obama. A Happy Meal toy is not Joe Camel [a cartoonish cigarette advertising character]. The toy, in and of itself, is not a gateway ticket to obesity. I'm not even sure a Happy Meal is a one-way trip to diabetes.

So what's the point of banning the toys in Happy Meals? What about the movie tie-in promotions aimed at children that aren't packaged with Happy Meals but are obviously meant to drag the young up to the caloric ordering counter? Because we are in a recession, shouldn't we require that poor parents sign an oath that the Dollar Value items will not be fed to their starving children? And does anyone seriously believe that a company like McDonald's won't figure out a way to keep kids coming in without the toys?

> **FAST FACT**
>
> A Stanford School of Medicine study found that the 2010 Santa Clara County, California, law that bans toy giveaways in unhealthy meals did not prompt restaurants to revamp their food recipes or add healthy foods to their menus.

If You Ban One, You Must Ban Thousands

But if we're being consistent—a rare trait in San Francisco legislative history—why not ban the prize in Crackerjacks? Why not require that any giveaway day for kids by the Giants [Major League Baseball team] should be coupled with a requirement that they be served tofu and salad at the ballpark? There must be a zillion ways that kids see or experience bad food choices, but this popgun approach only targets a single toy in a single product at a single fast food chain.

Preventing childhood obesity is about education, exercise, and alternatives. The First Lady [Michelle Obama] invites schoolchildren to her garden at the White House. [Chef] Alice Waters has created the Edible Schoolyard project. The NFL [National Football League] has its Play 60 program. You want to address the problem? Deal with an out-of-control budget that can't fund basic programs for kids that would get them off their duffs and away from the video consoles, and create healthier menus in schools. Things that make a difference in a kid's mind, body, and perceptions about his or her own health.

Attack the Problem, Not a Symbol

This proposal does none of these things. It is a symbolic law. Scratch that. It is a useless and symbolic law that will cost the City when McDonald's surely sues, coming at a time when public faith in government is at an all-time low. We have real problems in San Francisco for young people that go far beyond self-important press-grabbing social engineering experiments. We have young men in the Bayview and the Mission [low-income neighborhoods in San Francisco] who need alternatives to gangs; we have kids who go to bed hungry every night; we have too many children who don't have access to afterschool music or art or sports or theater because we can't figure out how to fund them.

Childhood obesity is a real problem requiring real solutions. But to blame it on a toy in a Happy Meal is a cheap—and ultimately fruitless—endeavor.

EVALUATING THE AUTHOR'S ARGUMENTS:

In this viewpoint Michael Yaki argues that banning toys from fast-food meals is an empty symbolic gesture that will not improve childhood obesity. In the previous viewpoint the Center for Science in the Public Interest argues it is wrong to pair toys with unhealthy food, especially because children do not have defenses against this type of marketing. After reading both viewpoints, with which author do you agree? What piece of evidence swayed you? It could be the identity of an author, a fact or opinion expressed in the viewpoint, or another piece of evidence.

Fast-Food Restaurants Should Be Required to Post Their Products' Nutrition Information

"People want to know what they're eating."

Margo Wootan

In the following viewpoint Margo Wootan argues that posting the calorie content of restaurant dishes helps consumers make healthier choices. She says if people only ate in restaurants occasionally, menu labeling would not have a big impact on their diet. But most Americans eat out nearly every day of the week, so the calories they get from restaurant meals constitute a large part of their total calorie intake. In addition, restaurant portions tend to be large and have more calories than home-cooked meals. Therefore, Wootan asserts, restaurant meals significantly contribute to the nation's growing obesity rate, and thus it makes sense to require restaurants to post nutritional content. She says people want to be aware that the food they eat has more calories, fat, or sugar than they would have guessed; when presented with the numbers, they are more likely to make healthy choices. She concludes that providing people with information leaves them free to order whatever they like, but it is likely they will make better decisions when armed with information. Wootan is the director of nutrition policy at the Center for Science in the Public Interest, a nonprofit organization that advocates for nutrition, health, food safety, alcohol policy, and sound science.

AS YOU READ, CONSIDER THE FOLLOWING QUESTIONS:
1. How many days a week does the average American eat out, according to Wootan?
2. About how many more calories do women who eat out more than five times per week consume on average each day than women who eat out less often?
3. What did a Stanford University study find about the effect of menu labeling at Starbucks cafés on people's purchases and calorie intake?

A 500-calorie bagel with cream cheese on your way to work. A 700-calorie sandwich for lunch, plus an extra 150 calories if you get chips instead of carrots on the side. A 400-calorie afternoon coffee drink. A 350-calorie margarita after work. And a 1,500-calorie chicken quesadilla with friends for dinner.

It's easy to see why obesity rates are so high—dozens of studies show that eating out more frequently is associated with obesity.

Restaurant Meals Pack on Calories

The average American, who should consume about 2,000 calories a day, eats out six times a week. That's enough to lead to over-consuming calories not just on the days a person eats out, but also to exceed calorie requirements over the course of the whole week. One study found that women who eat out more than five times a week consume about 290 more calories on average each day than women who eat out less often.

Big portions in restaurants mean we often get a lot more food than we realize, or than we may want or need. It's tough to accurately estimate the calorie content of popular restaurant foods, even for dietitians. Who can tell that a cinnamon roll (510 calories) has more than double the calories in a glazed donut (220), or that a typical tuna salad sandwich has almost 50 percent more calories (720) than a roast beef sandwich (460)?

The high calorie counts of restaurant foods didn't matter so much when eating out was an occasional treat. Going out to a restaurant was a big deal when I was young, and not just because I have 10 brothers and sisters. In the 1970s, families spent about a third of their food dollars on away-from-home foods. Today, it's about half. Given the growing role of restaurant food in our diets, what we eat at restaurants affects our health more than in the past.

People Want to Know What They Are Eating

To help people make informed choices at restaurants, we worked with Sen. Tom Harkin (D-Iowa) and Rep. Rosa DeLauro (D-Conn.) to pass a national menu-labeling policy in 2010. The law requires calories

McDonald's Corporation's website lists the nutritional value of its menu items.

Nutrition Facts	Serving Size	Calories	Calories from Fat	Total Fat (g)	% Daily Value**	Saturated Fat (g)	% Daily Value**	Trans Fat (g)	Cholesterol (mg)	% Daily Value**	Sodium (mg)	% Daily Value**	Carbohydrates (g)	% Daily Value**	Dietary Fiber (g)	% Daily Value**	Sugars (g)	Protein (g)	Vitamin A	Vitamin C
dwiches																				
ourger	3.5 oz (100 g)	250	80	9	13	3.5	16	0.5	25	9	520	22	31	10	2	6	6	12	0	2
seburger	4 oz (114 g)	300	110	12	19	6	28	0.5	40	13	750	31	33	11	2	7	6	15	6	2
eburger	5.8 oz (165 g)	440	210	23	35	11	54	1.5	80	26	1150	48	34	11	2	8	7	25	10	2
ble	5.3 oz (151 g)	390	170	19	29	8	42	1	65	22	920	38	33	11						
7 oz																				

Above the Vitamin A / Vitamin C columns: % DA

be listed on menus and menu boards at chain restaurants with 20 or more outlets. Like few policies today, the provision was bipartisan, and it had strong support from not only public health groups, but also the restaurant industry.

The Food and Drug Administration proposed sensible menu-labeling regulations in April 2011 and was expected to finalize them by the end of that year. Yet two years after the law's enactment, most Americans are still unable to make informed choices when eating out.

Some conservatives are railing against all regulation, and the [Barack Obama] administration is being overly cautious as the [2012 presidential] election approaches. But people want to know what they're eating. A recent poll found that 80 percent of Americans want menu labeling in restaurants, supermarkets and other purveyors of prepared food. State and local menu-labeling policies in Vermont, Philadelphia and Seattle have been popular with customers.

Menu Labeling Leads to Better Choices

Other state and local policies are on hold until the administration finalizes national regulations. They've passed their own menu-labeling laws, but are preempted from implementing anything different from the federal rules. In May [2012], Sens. Jeff Merkley (D-Ore.) and Ron Wyden (D-Ore.) wrote in a letter to the president, "We are pleased that menu labeling will be implemented nationally, but eager for Oregonians to benefit from expanded access to nutrition information as soon as possible."

Earlier this spring, 20 leading health groups called on the Obama administration to finalize the labeling rules and apply them to all restaurant-type foods and all menu items, as Congress intended.

Menu labeling will help improve Americans' diets and reduce their risk of obesity and other nutrition-related health problems. Studies

> **FAST FACT**
>
> In 2009 researchers from Yale recommended that menu-labeling laws be passed after they found that customers consumed fewer calories when ordering from menus that listed the calorie content of foods.

Menu Labeling Encourages Healthier Eating

A 2010 study by researchers at the University of Washington found that posting nutrition information of children's meal items had a significant impact on what parents ordered for their children. When parents saw calorie counts, they ordered about 20 percent fewer calories for their children.

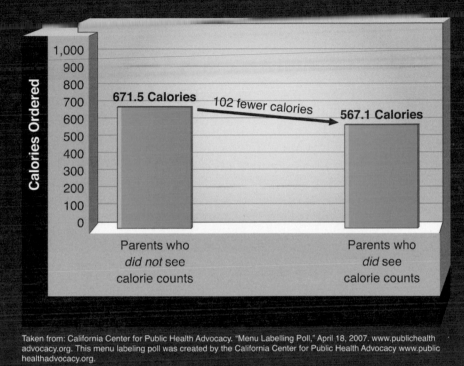

Taken from: California Center for Public Health Advocacy. "Menu Labelling Poll," April 18, 2007. www.publichealth advocacy.org. This menu labeling poll was created by the California Center for Public Health Advocacy www.public healthadvocacy.org.

show that providing nutrition information at restaurants can help people make lower-calorie choices. The biggest study, one by Stanford University researchers of Starbucks cafés, found that menu labeling reduced calories in customers' purchases by 6 percent. If people make similar changes in other chain restaurants—and an estimated 25 percent of calories consumed come from chains—that would mean a decrease of 30 calories per person per day, population-wide. Not bad, given that the obesity epidemic is explained by an imbalance of less than 100 calories per day. Calorie labeling also will encourage restaurants to add more low-calorie options and reduce calories in other items.

People Have the Right to Know

Without clear, easy-to-find calorie labeling, it's tough to make informed choices for what is a growing and often problematic part of our diets. It's time for the administration to finalize sensible menu-labeling regulations so people are free to make up their own minds about how many calories they really want to eat when eating out.

EVALUATING THE AUTHOR'S ARGUMENTS:

Imagine that on most days of the week, you have lunch at the same fast-food restaurant, where you order a burger, French fries, and cookies. Then imagine you were presented with information showing that your burger had 550 calories and 29 grams of fat, your French fries had 230 calories and 11 grams of fat, and your cookies had 160 calories and 8 grams of fat. Would you still order your regular meal? Or would you be likely to order something with fewer calories and less fat? Explain your decision.

Posting Fast-Food Nutrition Information Makes Little Difference in What People Order

"People may notice calorie counts on menu boards but, so far, few use the data to make significant changes to their orders."

Monica Eng

Monica Eng is a reporter for the *Chicago Tribune*. In the following viewpoint she reports that laws that require restaurants to post the nutrition content of their dishes do not significantly impact what people order. Most people who eat at fast-food restaurants are not interested in watching calories, she explains, or perhaps they want to indulge in fatty, sweet, or salty foods when they eat outside the home. Menu labeling is likely to appeal most to a health-conscious segment of society that is least likely to eat at fast-food restaurants to begin with. Numerous studies have shown that very few people consume fewer calories or make significantly different orders when confronted with the nutritional content of their dishes.

AS YOU READ, CONSIDER THE FOLLOWING QUESTIONS:
1. How does McDonald's customer Ron Offermann factor into the author's argument?
2. What percentage of customers visit restaurants primarily because they feature healthy or light menu items, according to Eng?
3. What percentage of teens say that nutritional information postings would affect what they order?

On a recent balmy afternoon Kristina Stefanopoulos was craving an Oreo McFlurry. But before she could order it she had to stare down its calorie count.

"I noticed that the snack size had only about 340 calories and the bigger one had more than 500," the 24-year-old Chicagoan said with a guilty laugh. "But I got the big one anyway."

People Want What They Want

Although she's concerned about calories and glad McDonald's started posting them on menus last week [mid-September 2012], Stefanopoulos said she really wanted the larger size.

It's a choice that echoes what several studies in New York and other early calorie-posting cities have reported: People may notice calorie counts on menu boards but, so far, few use the data to make significant changes to their orders.

This may not bode well for the national waistline, but it could reassure the nation's largest restaurant chains (those with more than 20 locations), which will likely have to disclose calories on menus later this year as part of the health care bill upheld by the Supreme Court.

Oak Brook [Illinois]–based McDonald's inspired headlines and applause last week for launching calorie listings before it was required. But studies and informal interviews with customers of the hamburger chain indicate that any risk of the calorie listings scaring away people or significantly cutting into sales may be minimal.

"I Don't Go to McDonald's to Count Calories"

Indeed, the chain's chief marketing officer, Neil Golden, says data from areas that require calorie postings (New York, Northern California and Seattle) indicates that the most prominent effect may be happier customers.

"We haven't seen any measurable shift in purchase patterns as a result," Golden said. "But in talking to customers we found that they are pleased and surprised to find that the choices they have always made fit easily within a healthy diet."

Ron Offermann, who recently ate lunch with co-workers at McDonald's, said the new listings wouldn't affect him.

"I don't go to McDonald's to count calories," said Offermann, 48. "When I go out to eat I don't worry about that at all."

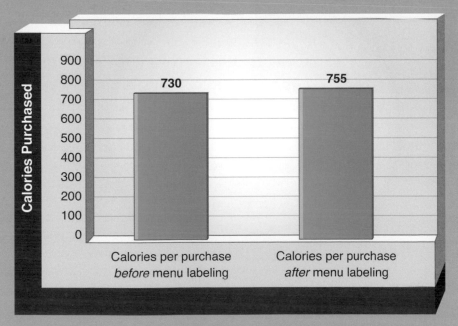

Menu Labeling Does Not Affect Teen Purchases

A study of teenage fast-food purchasing habits before and after mandatory labeling took effect in New York City found that labeling did not have a positive effect on what teens decided to eat. Although 57 percent said they noticed the label, only 9 percent said they considered the information when placing their order. In fact, on average, teens' calorie consumption went up *after* the labeling took effect.

Taken from: Kathleen Doheny. "Calorie Labels Don't Affect Kids' Fast-Food Choices." *U.S. News and World Report*, February 15, 2011. http://health.usnews.com/health:news/diet-fitness/diet/articles/2011/02/15/calorie-labels-dont-affect-kids-fast-food-choices.

NPD Group, a market research firm based in Port Washington, N.Y., said its analysis of data found most people share Offermann's view.

"When consumers eat out, they want to indulge and leave concerns about which foods are low-fat, low-calorie and low-sodium at home," the research firm said. "And in tough economic times, price concerns outweigh health concerns when it comes to eating out."

Menu Labeling Has Not Had Much Impact

To test how labeling might play out, last year NPD presented subjects with a regular hamburger restaurant menu and another that listed calories.

"What we found was that the impact was minimal," said NPD's restaurant industry analyst, Bonnie Riggs. "Consumers indicated they may be likely to change the size of their soft drink and french fries, but they are not willing to give them up entirely. We think (calorie counts) may have a small impact initially, but then consumers will just kind of go back to what they have always done."

Riggs noted NPD surveys indicate that only 9 percent of consumers cite "healthy" or "light" offerings as the primary reason for choosing a restaurant. The main reasons cited for patronizing fast-food restaurants is "convenience, price and to get a particular item. And so if that's the reason they went in there, (calorie counts) are not going to make a difference," Riggs said.

FAST FACT

A New York University study in *Health Affairs* revealed that people who were given fast-food menus that listed the products' calories did not choose items with fewer calories than did customers who ordered from standard menus.

Oleg Urminsky, who studies consumer decision-making, said he supports calorie disclosures but said some consumers ignore them.

"It can be very difficult to pass up the immediate benefit for the long-term reward, which is often well into the future and not felt as urgently," said Urminsky, an associate marketing professor at the

Opponents of published nutritional information say it is ineffective because people will order what they want regardless of nutritional guidelines.

Booth School of Business at the University of Chicago. "This is one part of what makes these health issues so difficult. People think, 'Right now I can have something really delicious and enjoyable and if I forgo it, over the next 20 years I might have slightly better health, so I'll have it just this once.'"

Calorie Listings Affect Those Who Need Them Least

Urminsky says that the calorie listings may have the most impact on those who may need them least: "Those are people who are already fairly health conscious and understand how many calories a healthy lunch should have," he said. "But I am not sure how many of them eat at McDonald's in the first place."

Still, some consumer studies on the subject are more hopeful than others.

For example, the NPD test with two menus (one with calories and one without) indicated that people might modify their orders to the tune of 100 calories in response to the calorie listings.

But when New York University [NYU] researchers tallied receipts from actual restaurant purchases the calorie difference evaporated. Another NYU study that focused on teens and parents buying for children showed that only 9 percent of teens said the data would influence their choices, while 28 percent of adults said it would. Neither group, however, made significant changes.

A Modest Difference, If Any

The most positive study on the topic, sponsored by the Robert Wood Johnson Foundation and the city of New York, indicated that calorie counts led 1 in 6 consumers to notice and act on the information. Average calorie reductions, the study said, ranged from 44 to 80, depending on the restaurant. Overall calorie consumption by participants, however, did not decrease.

While some view these small calorie modifications as failed public policy, Margo Wootan, director of nutrition policy at the Washington-based Center for Science in the Public Interest, said they make her "dance around my office."

She notes that the causes of obesity are multifaceted and the difference between obesity and healthy weight is about 100 calories (the amount burned by running a mile) a day. So if one public intervention can reduce 40 to 80 calories in some diners it can make a big difference.

Wootan says another major aim of calorie labeling was to force chains to take a hard look at the calorie content of its foods—which, she says, only about 50 percent had done—and consider reformulation on items that were embarrassingly high. She cites a recent University of Washington study saying that since calorie listing kicked in, the average entree in the Seattle area has dropped by about 40 calories.

Whether or not they believed it would make a difference in American health, most consumers surveyed outside a Chicago McDonald's said they liked knowing the information was there, and one said it was used in making a food choice.

"I was going to go for the Quarter Pounder," said Chris Nigro, of Chicago, holding up a chicken-scented bag. "But when I saw the calories I went for the chicken sandwich instead."

Fast-Food Ads Should Be Banned During Children's Programming

Kathy Chapman

> "It's time to stop undermining parents' influence over their children's eating habits."

Fast-food ads should not be shown during children's television shows, argues Kathy Chapman in the following viewpoint. Chapman explains that children are very vulnerable to commercials and other forms of marketing—their brains cannot yet tell fact from fiction, and they end up blindly wanting the foods shown to them on TV. Although fast-food restaurants promised to regulate the kinds and number of ads they would show to children, Chapman says they have done a terrible job: Since the industry began voluntarily regulating itself, the number of total ads has exponentially increased. Chapman is not surprised that an industry would fail to voluntarily sell less of its product. This is why, she states, the government needs to create mandatory regulations that restrict fast-food advertising during children's programs. Chapman is the health strategies director for the organization Cancer Council NSW, which works to promote cancer prevention in Australia.

AS YOU READ, CONSIDER THE FOLLOWING QUESTIONS:
1. According to Chapman, how many fast-food ads does a child who watches three hours of TV per day see?
2. What did the World Health Organization recommend regarding advertising standards for children?
3. What percentage of parents believe children should be protected from fast-food marketing, according to Chapman?

F ast food companies have failed to clean up their act under voluntary self regulations, with the total number of fast food ads increasing on television since 2009, and no change in children's exposure to unhealthy fast food ads. It proves what many of us feared: that the industry only pays lip service to effective and responsible advertising.

Kids Are Bombarded with Fast Food Ads

Recent research we undertook (*Medical Journal of Australia*) shows that children who watch up to three hours of television per day are

Kids See Thousands of Fast-Food Ads Each Year

Kids see thousands of fast-food ads on television each year. The vast majority are for menu items that are laden with salt, fat, sugar, or other unhealthy ingredients.

Restaurant	Advertising Spending (in millions)	Ages 2–5	Ages 6–11	Ages 12–17
All fast food*	$4188.8	1,021	1,272	1,723

*Figures are for advertising by McDonald's, Subway, Wendy's, Burger King, KFC, Taco Bell, Pizza Hut, Sonic, Domino's, Dunkin' Donuts, and Dairy Queen.

Taken from: The Nielsen Company (2010) / Nourish Interactive. www.nourishinteractive.com/healthy-living/free-nutrition-articles/187-fast-food-restaurant-advertising-kids.

exposed to more than 1640 fast food ads per year—a jump of more than 430 ads per year since industry regulations were introduced in August 2009.

This is contrary to the recommendations put forward by the World Health Organisation that any standards should be to reduce children's exposure to fast-food and unhealthy food and drink advertising.

Does this come as a surprise? Not really.

Fast Food Is Not a "Family Meal"

When seven major fast food companies established the Australian Quick Service Restaurant Industry Initiative for Responsible Advertising and Marketing to Children (QSRI) in August 2009 it was to appease community concern on fast food advertising to children.

> **FAST FACT**
>
> Since 1980 Quebec Province in Canada has prohibited all advertising targeted to kids under thirteen years old. The University of British Columbia claims that this ban reduced kids' likelihood of eating fast food by 13 percent and resulted in Quebec having the lowest obesity rate in Canada.

However, this self-regulation only applies to a very narrow range of advertised foods. These regulations, for example, don't cover "family meals" sold by fast food outlets which will be eaten by both parents and their children. A loophole the industry no doubt takes advantage of.

But let's face it; junk food companies have a vested interest in increasing profits from their products, and allowing the food industry to self regulate is like leaving the fox in charge of the henhouse.

Kids Need Protection from Relentless Messaging

And so junk food ads targeting children will continue to slip through regulatory loopholes and pass subjective and ineffective restrictions— all to the detriment of our children. The consistent scientific evidence shows us that food marketing influences what children want and what they ultimately eat and drink.

Surely it's time for this sugar coated voluntary code to be scrapped and replaced with clear and meaningful Government regulations that protect children at times they are actually watching television (not just limited to after school!) and reduce their exposure to the wrong types of food.

Fast-food companies spend an enormous amount of money advertising directly to kids. Parents say they cannot win against such influence.

Stop Undermining Parents

It's time to stop undermining parents' influence over their children's eating habits. Parents are up against an unchecked, marketing-savvy, multimillion dollar junk food industry and it's not surprising that more than eight out of ten parents believe children should be protected from this type of marketing.

With one in four Australian children being overweight or obese—it's critical as a society we stop putting profit ahead of our health.

EVALUATING THE AUTHOR'S ARGUMENTS:

Kathy Chapman says parents cannot win when they are up against enormous fast-food companies that are well-funded, marketing-savvy, and intent on selling their product to kids. How might parents be able to counter the influence the fast-food companies' marketing tactics have on their children? List at least three ways.

Chapter 3

Should Restrictions Be Placed on Fast Food?

A fast-food related controversy has arisen around attempts to ban large soda drinks in places such as New York City.

A Tax for Health

Julia M. Gallo-Torres

"Ditching sugary drinks or foods seems like [an] . . . easy way to cut many extra calories."

Julia M. Gallo-Torres is category manager at Foodservice-US and formerly was a managing editor at *Prepared Foods* with BNP Media. In the following viewpoint Gallo-Torres accepts the findings of an article by the US Department of Agriculture's Economic Research Service (ERS) that suggests a tax of at least 20 percent on sugary beverages would curb people's desire both to drink such beverages and to get around efforts to remove such beverages from people's diet.

AS YOU READ, CONSIDER THE FOLLOWING QUESTIONS:
1. According to the viewpoint, a study by what institution found that eliminating sodas from vending machines was ineffective as a means of addressing childhood obesity?
2. According to the viewpoint, in the study just mentioned, what percentage of students from schools with soda-bans drank sodas? What percentage of students from schools with no soda-bans drank sodas?
3. As stated in the article, how many pounds would an adult lose per year as a result of a 20 percent tax on sugary drinks? How many pounds would a child lose per year?

Poor soda. It has gone from being a refreshing drink, associated with images of people empowered to enjoy life, to something we no longer should serve our children. Last year, a study by the Yale School of Public Health found that trying to address childhood obesity by eliminating sodas from vending machines was not effective. I was amused, when I read the kids who did not have access to vending machines in schools had no trouble getting their hands on sugary drinks. "In schools that allow access to soft drinks, 86% of the students reported consumption within the past week," stated the article, which ran in *Prepared Foods*' E-dition e-newsletter last year. However, in schools without access, a hefty 84% of the students still drank the beverages. Kids can be very resourceful, when it comes to things they want.

In my mind, this behavior parallels smoking and smokers. Smoking was banned in school, but the smokers could always be found sneaking their habit somewhere on school grounds. Furthermore, all the taxes smokers have endured still do not make it any easier for them to quit. So, to me, it seems a soda tax would not work. However, it turns out I'm wrong. An article in this month's issue (page 25), by the USDA's Economic Research Service (ERS), reports that a tax of at least 20% on sugary beverages, an increase that directly hits consumers, is needed to result in change. Taking various factors into account, the report states consumers would then choose bottled water first, followed by other beverages, such as juice and diet drinks.

> **FAST FACT**
>
> In 2010 experts at the University of North Carolina–Chapel Hill declared that an 18 percent tax to discourage people from consuming fast food and soda would cause them to lose up to five pounds per year, lessening their chance of developing weight-related diseases.

Based on this ERS study, the changes would "translate into an average loss per year of 3.8 lbs for adults and 4.5 lbs for children." Perhaps these figures do not seem like much, but Americans between the ages of 25–55 gain about 1.5 lbs per year. Ditching sugary drinks or foods seems like a straightforward, easy way to cut many extra calories, slowing the path to obesity. (Logically, this will only work, if people do not eat extra foods or beverages that will "make up" for the saved calories.)

Making sugary drinks harder for children to obtain is just a beginning; apparently, adults need deterrents, also. I was very glad to hear the collected taxes would be used to fund education programs promoting weight management strategies. A more focused health education can help both children and adults learn how to best take care of their bodies.

EVALUATING THE AUTHOR'S ARGUMENTS:

The author of the viewpoint, Julia M. Gallo-Torres, supports the claim of the articles in USDA's Economic Research Service that a 20 percent tax on soda would result in Americans losing over 3 lbs per year. Are you convinced by the claim? Explain why or why not.

Soda Should Not Be Taxed

David Gratzer

A tax on unhealthful products like soda would not reduce obesity or raise meaningful amounts of money, argues David Gratzer in the following viewpoint. He argues that taxes that focus on soda miss the point of the obesity problem. Soda and sugary drinks are consumed by a minority of the population and are not a main contributor to obesity. Taxing them, therefore, would unfairly punish one product over others. Gratzer also warns that a tax on sugar-sweetened beverages would also end up including other beverages that are actually healthy, such as juices, teas, and milks. Finally, Gratzer argues that if sugary beverages are taxed, people will not suddenly start drinking more water or other healthy beverages—they are more likely to replace their soda with something just as bad for their health. For all of these reasons he concludes that a tax on sugar-sweetened beverages is an ineffective solution to the obesity problem. Gratzer is a physician, author, and senior fellow at the Montreal Economic Institute.

> "There is little evidence . . . that a Canadian soda tax would be anything more than a politically-motivated tax, arbitrarily levied on a convenient scapegoat."

David Gratzer, "Are Soda Taxes a Cure for Obesity?," Montreal Economic Institute, November 2012.

AS YOU READ, CONSIDER THE FOLLOWING QUESTIONS:
  1. What foods did the National Health and Nutrition
     Examination Survey (NHANES) find were higher in calories
     than soda, energy, and sports drinks combined?
  2. According to Gratzer, eating less of which food would have a
     larger impact on weight loss than soda?
  3. What does the phrase "calorific substitution" mean in the con-
     text of the viewpoint?

I n early 2012, a spokesperson for [Canadian] Federal Health
Minister Leona Aglukkaq rejected the idea of a Canada-wide
soda tax. Still, a Public Health Agency of Canada poll released
this year [2012] found that 40% of Canadians would support a soda
tax if funds raised were used to fight childhood obesity. Is there any
indication that such a tax would be effective?

Tax Predictions Are Overly Optimistic

Soda tax proponents generally call for an excise tax, imposed directly
on manufacturers and wholesalers of sugar-sweetened beverages. In a
widely-cited 2009 paper in the *New England Journal of Medicine*, Dr.
Kelly Brownell and other proponents of a tax on sweetened beverages
argued that an excise tax would be "simpler to administer" than a retail
tax. A retail tax would be less effective, since it would only raise the
cost to consumers after the purchase decision was made.

For such a tax to have an impact, a given increase in price has to
lead to an appreciable fall in the overall quantity of soda demanded by
consumers, which *must* in turn lead to population-wide weight loss.
This is the basic assumption of soda tax proponents. Dr. Brownell
projects that a modest tax would cut net U.S. calorie intake "by a
minimum of 20 kcal [kilocalories] per person per day." A study by
the U.S. Department of Agriculture projects an average weight loss of
roughly four pounds over a year from a 20% soda tax. A 2012 estimate
in *Health Affairs* projects that a smaller tax should lead to enough
weight loss to extend 26,000 lives over a ten-year period.

These projections have been disputed by other scientists because
they are too broad and are based on methodologically weak assump-

tions. In a *Lancet* article, researchers explain that public health advocates usually overstate the potential weight loss estimates from anti-obesity policy interventions, because they rarely take into account the fact that a person's metabolism will adjust to minor reductions in calorie intake. However, optimistic assumptions are not the main problem with these scenarios.

Too Narrow in Focus

Even if consumers were really going to cut their consumption of soda and other sweetened beverages appreciably following a price increase, several limitations make soda taxation a poor policy choice. The first one is the excessively narrow focus of such a tax.

Soda critics often cite a particular U.S. study in a manner that overstates soda's share of the problem. For example, a Canadian anti-soda organization's website claimed that "a 2004 study found that soft drinks are the largest single contributor of caloric intake in the US." This is untrue.

In fact, the study in question was the National Health and Nutrition Examination Survey (NHANES). The survey's 2003 2004 data and subsequent reports found that soda was just one unhealthy component among many, when consumed in too large quantities, in the American diet. Grain-based desserts, yeast breads, as well as chicken and chicken mixed dishes all provide a higher share of dietary calories than did soda, energy and sport drinks combined in the 2005–2006 NHANES data. The latter accounted for 5.3% of total calorie intake. A separate 2011 study of dietary changes finds that cuts to potato chip or potato intake were associated with greater weight loss than a similar reduction in soda intake.

Sugary Beverages Are No Worse than Other Foods

Canadians for their part get less than 2.5% of their calories from soft drinks. In most age and gender categories, Canadian adults consume more coffee or beer than soft drinks. A large Tim Hortons [restaurant chain] "double-double" coffee has 270 calories, while a "triple-triple" has 405 calories. The chain's popular iced cappuccino rings in at 470 calories for a large serving with cream. By comparison, a 591 ml bottle of sugar-sweetened Coca-Cola (equivalent to a large cup of coffee) has 260 calories.

Measured on a calories-to-volume basis, these three Tim Hortons drinks are therefore more "sugary" than a bottle of Coca-Cola. But only one—the iced cappuccino—would presumably be taxable under an excise tax model, since sugar and cream are added at the point of sale for the others.

Another reason activists like to focus on soda and sweetened beverages is that they are a large source of *added* sugar, that is, refined calorie-containing sweeteners added to foods and beverages during processing or preparation. However, obesity is not caused by "added sugar" or "wasted calories." Such terms create a false impression. Given that pizza is rich in sodium and solid fats, 400 calories worth of pizza with "no added sugar" could easily be less healthy than the same calories from a large soda.

A Tax Would Catch Healthy Products, Too

Another limitation is that even if we wanted to broaden the scope of the tax, it would be difficult to target the right types of drink.

Taxing the manufacture of all sweetened drinks—the preferred solution of most soda tax advocates—would also capture non-carbonated drinks, including flavored milks, sweetened teas, fruit smoothies or otherwise healthy juices like sweetened cranberry juice. Beverages that contain essential nutrients (including calcium, vitamin C and vitamin E) would be taxed. Lawmakers could avoid this dilemma by taxing only carbonated beverages. However, this would leave many calories out of the intervention.

New York City has seen this dilemma in action on a related issue: serving size regulation. As drafted, the new regulation banning any sweetened beverage over 16 fluid ounces has several unintended consequences. One key flaw is how sweetness is defined. The rules define "sweetened" to mean any drink that has more than 25 calories per 8-ounce serving.

FAST FACT

A CBS News poll conducted in 2009 revealed that the majority of Americans—60 percent—do not think there should be a tax on fast foods.

Protesters in Philadelphia demonstrate against a two-cent-per-ounce tax on sodas.

As the co-founder of the Honest Tea line of beverages explained, the company's most popular product is an organic Honey Green Tea, which contains 35 calories per 8 ounces in a 16.9-ounce bottle. The slogan, "Just a Tad Sweet" is printed right on the bottle. The company selected this serving size because it was standard for nearby bottlers. Honest Tea can now either take its (low-calorie) tea out of the New York City market, or it can retool its entire production line and distribution system to sell bottles that are a bit smaller, all because its product has only a few more calories per unit than an arbitrary sweetness threshold. One way or another, this won't reduce the rate of obesity in New York City.

Consumers Will Likely Choose Another Bad Food

All other things being equal, a consumer who is only encouraged to cut soda calories is likely to replace them with other foods and beverages. This is known as "calorific substitution." Soda tax proponents often understate this problem, and their estimates vary widely. In 2009, Dr. Brownell's "conservative estimate" was a calorific substitution rate of 25%. Others assume a 40% substitution rate.

Other studies of substitution rates are more pessimistic. One finds that substitution effects are so complex that poorly targeted food and beverage taxes [as written by C. Schroeter et al.] "could actually increase weight." Other researchers [Jason Fletcher et al.] found that each additional 1% increase in state soft drink tax rates led "to a decrease in body mass index (BMI) of 0.003 points"—basically a rounding error. Even a very large tax increase might therefore have no perceivable effect. The problem [according to Fletcher et al.] is that the "reduction in soda consumption is completely offset by increases in consumption of other high-calorie drinks."

Taxes Pose Political Problems

To cut soda consumption, any tax must be high enough to shift consumer behavior—yet higher taxes reduce the likelihood of political approval. Dr. Brownell and his colleagues called for a tax of one penny per sweetened fluid ounce. In Canada, this formula would raise the price of a standard can of soda by $0.12 per can, roughly 10%. Most observers argue that any anti-obesity tax would have to increase prices by 20% or more to significantly change behavior.

Recession-battered American voters haven't shown much enthusiasm for proposed soda taxes. In 2010, 60% of Washington State voters overturned soda, candy and bottled water taxes in a ballot initiative; the target of their wrath was an excise tax of just two cents per twelve ounces. British Columbia's HST [harmonized sales tax] backlash suggests Canadian voters could prove to be just as testy about proposals to raise consumer taxes, which, it should be noted, will hit lots of people who consume only moderate quantities of soda.

Higher taxes may also not deliver expected levels of higher prices for every product. Beverage companies will try to protect market share with discounts, loyalty programs, and other promotions. Governments would have to fix prices to counter this problem, again

Americans increasingly frown upon "sin taxes," or taxes on products like fast food and junk food. A 2012 poll by Rasmussen Reports found 63 percent of Americans opposed taxes on junk food. Just 18 percent supported the idea.

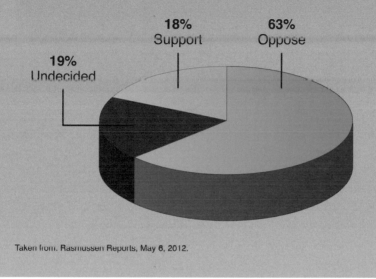

18%
Support

63%
Oppose

19%
Undecided

Taken from: Rasmussen Reports, May 8, 2012.

raising the political difficulty of controlling consumer, taxpayer and corporate behaviours in order to attain uncertain goals.

A Poor Fix to a Real Problem

While heavy-handed taxes and regulations are popular in public health circles, there are better, more constructive options. American and British experiments have shown that positive financial incentives can be more effective at motivating people to achieve dietary and weight loss goals. We must also train and organize primary care providers to help patients see obesity as a preventable medical risk. Students are a captive market when it comes to school meals and school schedules. Public health advocates are right to demand healthier school meals and a return to regular physical education.

The obesity problem is real. There is little evidence, though, that a Canadian soda tax would be anything more than a politically-motivated tax, arbitrarily levied on a convenient scapegoat.

EVALUATING THE AUTHOR'S ARGUMENTS:

David Gratzer is a doctor. Given his background, does it surprise you that he would argue against a tax on products like soda? If so, why? If not, why not? Use evidence from the text in your answer.

Fast Food Should Be Banned Near Schools

Micah White

"We have scientific evidence that fast food near schools results in student obesity."

In the following viewpoint Micah White argues that fast-food restaurants and other junk-food vendors should be banned near schools. He discusses research showing that when fast-food restaurants are close to schools, students experience higher rates of obesity. Students make choices based on what is convenient and tastes good, but they rarely think about their health, he says. Thus, putting fast-food restaurants near their schools is like putting flames near moths: Students are compulsively drawn to the sugar, fat, salt, and social connections they make with other teens who hang out there. Since childhood obesity is a crisis, White says it is irresponsible to allow junk-food peddlers anywhere near schools. In the same way gun-free and drug-free zones have been established around schools, so too should governments establish fast-food–free zones. White is a contributing editor at *Adbusters*, a newsmagazine and website based in British Columbia that reports on how commercial forces degrade social, physical, and cultural environments.

I was recently driving past a public high school during its lunch break when I witnessed a troubling sight. A hungry horde of teens was streaming out the doors of the school and looking for a place to eat. A quick glance about the area revealed their limited options: a McDonald's across the street or a Taco Bell a block further away. If those two options didn't appeal, there was always the local convenience store with frozen microwavable options.

I wondered about the long-term consequences of allowing a fast food "restaurant" to open within walking distance of a school. Now, thanks to the work of economists at the University of California, Berkeley and Columbia University, we have scientific evidence that fast food near schools results in student obesity. Could these findings be the beginning of a movement to ban fast food near our children's schools?

> **FAST FACT**
>
> According to researchers at the University of California, Berkeley, high school freshmen are more likely to be obese if their school is within a tenth of a mile from a fast-food restaurant, and limiting such restaurants near schools could significantly reduce obesity rates.

Proving What We Already Know

Sometimes it takes a detailed scientific study to prove what we already knew. This eight-year study looked at the weight of over three million school children and a million pregnant women. The researchers concluded that "among 9th grade children, a fast food restaurant within a tenth of a mile of a school is associated with at least a 5.2 percent increase in obesity rate" and for pregnant women "a fast food restaurant within a half mile of her residence results in a 2.5 percent increase in the probability of gaining over 20 kilos."

What is interesting about this study is that it provides culture jammers with a concrete, reasonable and accomplishable goal for improving the health of children. As the researchers point out, there is no

Fast-Food Restaurants Near Schools Impact Child Obesity

A study reported in the *American Journal of Preventative Medicine* examined the proximity of fast-food restaurants to schools in Chicago, Illinois. It reported that the majority of schools had at least one fast-food restaurant within half a mile. The median distance from any school to the nearest fast-food restaurant was about a third of a mile, a walking distance of about five minutes. The authors concluded that concentrating fast-food restaurants within a short walking distance from schools exposes children to poor-quality food environments and contributes to childhood obesity.

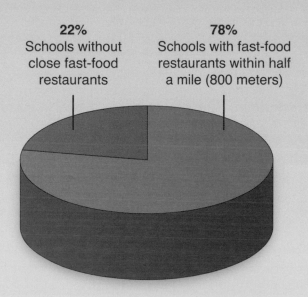

22%
Schools without close fast-food restaurants

78%
Schools with fast-food restaurants within half a mile (800 meters)

Taken from: S. Bryn Austin et al. "Clustering of Fast-Food Restaurants Around Schools: A Novel Application of Spatial Statistics to the Study of Food Environments." *American Journal of Public Health*, vol. 95, no. 9, September 2005, pp. 1575–1581.

A Burger King stands across the street from Orr High School in Chicago. Studies have shown that a fast-food restaurant within a tenth of a mile of a school increases child obesity rates by 5.2 percent.

discernible effect on obesity when the fast food restaurants are located further than ¼ miles from the school entrance. We could see a substantial decrease in childhood obesity by simply moving fast food restaurants a mere 400 meters from schools.

We Need a "Drug-Free Zone" for Fast Food

There is historical precedent for this type of campaign. Anti-noise activists inspired by [professor] Theodor Lessing around the turn of the 20th century, for example, were successful in introducing clauses into city ordinances that require quiet within a certain distance of schools and hospitals. These laws continue to persist in the books in many cities across the States (including my own state, New York). In the States there is also a mandated "Drug Free Zone" around schools. And, according to the *Los Angeles Times*, LA already "has a one-year moratorium on new fast-food outlets in a 32-square-mile area of South LA."

A few vocal citizens in communities across the world can immediately decrease childhood obesity simply by stating the obvious: kids need healthy food. We can launch a movement for "Healthy Food Zones" within 400 meters of all schools. In these areas, only local restaurants that provide healthy options to children and students will be tolerated.

EVALUATING THE AUTHOR'S ARGUMENTS:

Like many other authors in this book, Micah White compares fast food to drugs or guns. Specifically, he suggests that just as schools are designated as a gun-free or drug-free zone, so too should they be designated as fast- food–free zones. What do you think of this idea? Is fast food on par with guns or drugs? Should schools require such merchants to operate a certain distance from their schools? Why or why not?

Fast Food Should Not Be Banned Near Schools

> "If high schools want to steer students clear of junk-food lunches, they should require them to stay on campus during the school day."

Los Angeles Times

In the following viewpoint editors at the *Los Angeles Times* argue that fast-food restaurants and other junk-food vendors should not be banned near schools. They suggest the connection between fast food and childhood obesity is weak and possibly nonexistent. Given this, banning such vendors near schools is an overreaction to an unproven problem. If schools want to prevent students from eating fast food and junk food during the school day, they can require students to stay on campus and feed them healthy cafeteria lunches. But once the school day ends, students' diets are not the government's concern, say the editors. The authors conclude that childhood obesity is a multifaceted and complex problem, one that will not be solved by inappropriately inviting government into students' lives and putting harsh restrictions on businesses.

AS YOU READ, CONSIDER THE FOLLOWING QUESTIONS:

1. If the food bill in question passes, what do the authors say will be allowed closer to schools than fast- and junk-food vendors?
2. According to the authors, what did a 2007 study find about who accompanies students to fast- and junk-food vendors located near schools? What bearing does this have on their argument?
3. What did the Rand Corporation find about the link between childhood obesity and food environments, according to the authors?

New legislation in Sacramento [California's capital] that would ban food trucks and other street vendors from doing business within 1,500 feet of a school just doesn't pass the taste test. The purpose of the bill is to prevent childhood obesity, but that is a large and complicated problem, and the state isn't going to reverse obesity by controlling every aspect of a child's or a teenager's life.

Students Will Find Fast Food Somewhere

Certainly, the government is responsible for the well-being of children while they're in school. The [Barack] Obama administration has rightly taken strong steps to ensure that school meals are more wholesome than they used to be. Now schools need to take those rules and figure out how to produce appealing food that students are willing to eat.

We're not suggesting that food vendors aren't part of the problem. But the reality is that the more gourmet food trucks are less likely to park outside a school. The vendors that are there are often

> **FAST FACT**
>
> Fast-food restaurants outnumber elementary and secondary schools in the United States. According to the US Department of Education, during the 2009–2010 school year, there were 132,183 public and private schools in the United States. Meanwhile, the *Los Angeles Times* reports that there are more than 160,000 fast-food restaurant locations in the United States.

California tried to pass legislation banning food trucks near schools. The legislation met with opposition from many different quarters and was ultimately shelved.

selling out of strollers and coolers, and though some sell fruit, the big attractions are Flaming Hot Cheetos and sweetened drinks.

But will banning them force kids to eat healthily? If students don't have vendors close to hand, there's a good chance they'll find convenience stores and fast-food outlets within a few blocks that also sell unhealthful food. If the bill were to pass, even medical marijuana collectives could be located closer to schools than food vendors—600 feet.

Laws Are Getting Ahead of Science

A 2007 UCLA [University of California, Los Angeles] study of a few Los Angeles elementary schools found that children rush to the vendors outside the gates when school lets out. But more often than not, they are accompanied by parents or caregivers who buy them items. Other adults drive up to purchase snacks, the study reported. In other words, adults are frequently deciding whether and what the children may eat, and it's not clear why the state needs to step in to micromanage such decisions. Los Angeles, by the way, already bans vendors near schools, but the ban has limited effect, according to the study, because it's seldom enforced. A new state law is unlikely to change that.

Research is mixed on whether proximity to junk food and fast food is a major contributor to obesity. A new study from the Rand Corp. finds no real link between obesity in California's youngsters and their "food environments"—that is, close availability of fast food or supermarkets selling fresh food. But it didn't look at the immediate temptation of mobile food vendors. Attempts at policymaking are running ahead of solid research on what works.

Other School Policy Changes Make More Sense

Elementary school students already aren't allowed to leave campus for lunch, and if high schools want to steer students clear of junk-food lunches, they should require them to stay on campus during the school day. They also can ask parents not to give their children money for snack food. Once school is out of session, though, it's time for the government to bow out of personal food decisions.

EVALUATING THE AUTHOR'S ARGUMENTS:

In this viewpoint the *Los Angeles Times* editors use facts, research, examples, and reasoning to make their argument that fast-food restaurants and vendors should not be banned near schools. They do not, however, use any quotations to support their point. If you were to rewrite this article and insert quotations, what voices might you quote? Where would you place their comments, and why?

People Should Be Able to Spend Food Stamps on Fast Food

"The dollar menu suddenly looks like a reasonable option in many neighborhoods in Milwaukee."

Sherrie Tussler

Sherrie Tussler is executive director of the Hunger Task Force of Milwaukee in Wisconsin. In the following viewpoint she explains why she thinks people who receive food stamps should be allowed to spend them in fast-food restaurants. Poor people lack not only money, Tussler explains, but also access to food. Many live in neighborhoods that do not have grocery stores. Some live in dwellings that are without kitchens. Hunger therefore becomes not just a question of being able to afford certain foods, but a matter of being able to find food and prepare it. Fast-food restaurants—typically prevalent in poor neighborhoods—thus become a critical source of food stamp recipients' calories. Fast food is cheap, which means people on a very tight food stamp budget can afford it. Tussler says it is wrong to deny people already struggling to feed themselves this affordable and practical option. She thinks it is elitist to demand that poor people eat healthfully on incredibly tight resources. For all of these reasons, she thinks fast-food restaurants should be allowed to accept food stamps.

AS YOU READ, CONSIDER THE FOLLOWING QUESTIONS:
1. According to Tussler, what do Americans *not* expect hungry people to be?
2. What equipment do some food stamp recipients lack that Tussler says requires them to rely on restaurants for food?
3. How is food defined for government purposes, according to Tussler? What bearing does this have on her argument?

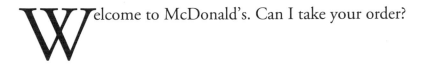

elcome to McDonald's. Can I take your order?

The Poor Should Have the Same Options as All of Us

Who among us hasn't heard that question? It seems that some of us believe that poor people should not hear it—that they should not be allowed to use their FoodShare benefits [food stamps] to purchase fast food. Some think it's bad because the food is unhealthy—"How can they be both hungry and fat?" "Why don't they spend their meager incomes more wisely?" and "Why doesn't government stop people from buying junk food?!"

As director of Milwaukee's free and local food bank and a lobbyist on anti-hunger public policy, I am often prodded to answer these questions.

Understanding the Hunger-Fat Paradox

People use the words "hunger" and "starvation" interchangeably. They expect that hungry people should appear like the ads on late-night TV where you can feed a child in a Third World country for 20 cents a day. Then they see an obese child at a local homeless shelter and feel angry because the child is overweight, not because the child is at a homeless shelter. (Whose child belongs at a homeless shelter?)

Children and adults who are fed a steady diet of starches, canned vegetables and processed foods will gain weight, but they will still get hungry three times a day. They can be both hungry and fat.

Hunger has two causes: lack of money for food and lack of access to food. Most people understand the money part. Understanding the lack of access issue would require spending time in a neighborhood different from your own.

It Is Not Just a Payment Issue

Your standard, big-box grocery store is not present in all neighborhoods. People rely on corner stores, gas stations and, yes, fast-food outlets in order to get food within walking distance of where they live. These corner stores can charge up to 40% more for food. Fresh vegetables, fruit and meat may not be on the shelves. Some folks getting FoodShare don't have a kitchen or the supplies to make food that requires any sort of preparation.

FAST FACT

According to the US Department of Agriculture's Food and Nutrition Service, there were 45 million participants in the Supplemental Nutrition Assistance Program in 2011—a record high.

Lots of us assume that everyone can jump in a car and run to the store; this just isn't an alternative for everyone, which is why federal food-stamp regulation allows a state option for the purchase of food at restaurants by seniors, people with disabilities and the homeless. Considering all of this, the dollar menu suddenly looks like a reasonable option in many neighborhoods in Milwaukee.

Food Remains a Matter of Choice, Even for the Poor

The question of government regulation is a complex one. We define "food" by its UPC code—FoodShare recipients can use their card to buy food but not liquor, tobacco or cleaning or paper products.

Food producers, restaurants and stores need and lobby for the broadest definition of food in order to make a profit. Imagine the regulatory effort implied in narrowing food choices for FoodShare

The author argues that since many poor people who depend on food stamps live in areas with no grocery stores and no kitchen facilities, food stamps should be able to be spent on fast food.

recipients to those that are either "healthy" or "proper." Then imagine the effort of food industry lobbyists to oppose regulation. Then think of the bill that would be delivered to the taxpayer in order to implement the new regulations. The mood of the voting public of late is for less, not more, government.

Food Stamp Use in the United States

Enrollment in the food stamp program was at a record high in 2011, with 14.6 percent of the total population relying on them. Some argue that letting these millions of people use food stamps to buy fast food is a realistic and practical solution to hunger and food access problems. The following map shows food stamp enrollment by state.

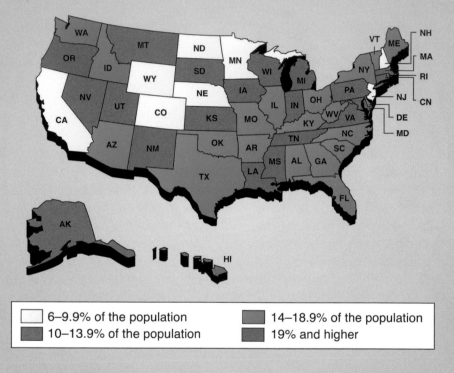

6–9.9% of the population
10–13.9% of the population
14–18.9% of the population
19% and higher

Taken from: Sara Murray. "About 1 in 7 in U.S. Receive Food Stamps." *Wall Street Journal*, May 3, 2011.

So who should choose what goes on your plate? You should. Should you choose what goes on another person's plate? If your answer is yes, I hope you are a registered dietitian, the lunch lady at school or, at the very least, the person in your house making dinner tonight.

Should FoodShare be accepted by restaurants in Wisconsin? I say yes—to bring access, choices and dignity to people. Will it happen in Wisconsin? Doubtful. I think our legislators have a full plate of something else they need to chew on.

People Should Not Be Able to Spend Food Stamps on Fast Food

Denise Williams

"Show me where ordering a No. 1 with cheese and a large Coke, paid for with tax dollars, is a constitutionally protected right."

Food stamps should not be spent on fast food, argues Denise Williams in the following viewpoint. Williams asserts that even the poor have many alternatives to fast food: Those without access to grocery stores can get healthy meals from shelters and halfway houses, and similar options exist for those who lack kitchens and cooking equipment. Williams says eating in a restaurant is a luxury, and one the poor unfortunately cannot afford. When she turned to food stamps, she was able to cook healthful but affordable meals for her family. Therefore, she knows firsthand that people on food stamps do not need to rely on fast-food, especially considering how unhealthy it is. She suggests that the push to let people use food stamps in fast-food restaurants is nothing more than a ploy by fast-food companies to add to their profits. Williams concludes the government should not be subsidizing poor people's fast-food indulgences. Williams is a columnist for the *Plainfield Patch*, an online community newspaper in Illinois.

AS YOU READ, CONSIDER THE FOLLOWING QUESTIONS:
1. How many people received food stamps as of October 2010?
2. What, according to the author, do fast-food companies see as an "untapped consumer market"?
3. What happened to the author on September 18, 2001? What bearing does it have on her argument?

S ome fast food restaurants are lobbying to get a piece of the Supplemental Nutrition Assistance Program [SNAP] pie. Most people are more familiar with SNAP being referred to as food stamps.

Their argument is that some disabled or homeless people cannot buy groceries and cook for themselves. They say they are trying to combat hunger among the poorest of the poor. They even argue that fast food is better than no food, which is the most disturbing and distorting of all the arguments I've heard.

Even the Poor Have Alternatives to Fast Food

First, the facts. Those who are disabled and unable to shop and cook for themselves already have a mechanism to use their food stamp allowances in restaurants.

Homeless shelters that cater to families have provisions for the family to use their food stamps to purchase food for the shelter to cook, and in some cases, access to kitchen areas for families to cook for themselves.

Other shelters, as well as half-way houses for felons, recovering addicts and those needing group supportive living, use the food stamps of the residents to feed those receiving shelter and services in their facilities.

In other words, the argument that there are populations who cannot use the food stamps for which they qualify in grocery stores is at best ridiculous and specious.

A mother prepares a meal at a homeless shelter. Opponents of using food stamps for fast-food purchases say that homeless shelters allow families to use food stamps to purchase food that the shelter will then prepare for them.

Fast Food Companies Just Want Food Stamp Dollars

This argument is designed to pull at the heart strings of the general public, who will then pressure their elected representatives to support this initiative. I'm not sure which idea is worse, the public weighing in without facts or politicians being that ignorant of the laws they are sworn to uphold.

Actually, the most disturbing idea of all is politicians caving in to these hysterical, unsubstantiated and blatantly false arguments to pander for votes. And secure lobbyist dollars.

Are there instances where families are trying to exist where they have no access to cooking facilities? Of course. But we don't and can't make the rules to cover the exception. The system is and must be set up to cover the majority, or the system comes crashing down.

This entire issue is nothing more [than] a few corporations attempting to add to their bottom line.

As of October 2010, a staggering 43.2 million people receive SNAP benefits. That is a huge and growing portion of the population, or in the eyes of these businesses, an untapped consumer market.

Assistance Should Be Spent on Healthy Foods

Now let's talk about the purpose and design of SNAP. The name pretty much says it all—Supplemental Nutrition Assistance Program. The formula basics are predicated on the equation that 30 percent of household expenditures are on food.

The very poorest households receive more dollars, to attempt to equalize the available dollars to be spent on food. The base line to qualify is at or below 130 percent of the poverty line, though there are provisions for those receiving unemployment and other forms of temporary aid such as short term disability. The rules disallowing single adults with no dependents have been suspended in most states due to the current economic crisis.

All of which is another way of saying there is a lot of money going to a lot of people to spend on food. But not fast food.

Fast food corporations are feeling the pinch of the economic squeeze, and their response is to pass along the pain to the taxpayer. To add insult to injury, they are pretending their motivation is concern over the growing hunger problem in America.

> **FAST FACT**
>
> According to the organization Eat, Drink, Politics, in 2011 the federal government spent $72 billion on Supplemental Nutrition Assistance Program expenditures. The organization argues that fast-food companies want food stamps to be accepted at their restaurants so they can access some of this money.

There really is no argument to the fact that most fast food is nutritionally deficit at best, when not flat-out unhealthy. There is also no argument to the fact that people can and do use food stamps in grocery stores for equally unhealthy choices.

Eating in Restaurants Is a Luxury, Not a Right

But, there is absolutely no valid argument to the fact that eating out in a restaurant, fast food or not, is not a right. It is a convenience and a luxury. Like all conveniences and luxuries, it is not something everyone can afford.

On Sept. 18, 2001, I was laid off from my job. There were simply no other jobs to be had. The entire country was frozen [after the September 11th terrorist attacks], waiting to see what would happen next. I did finally find a job that December, but I existed on unemployment compensation and food stamps for those months.

I had no savings to speak of, literally less than one month's bills in the bank. Those were scary times, and I feel for the hundreds of thousands of families across the country currently living through that nightmare.

Because of this experience, I know firsthand that it is not only possible, it was much easier than I expected to feed my family on food stamps. Like most people, I had heard the horror stories of not being able to buy enough food for the month on the allowance I was given. Granted, it meant changes in the way I cooked and what I bought, but we did not go hungry.

Potato chips, cookies and snack cakes, prime cuts of meat, the best vegetables and out of season fruit were among the first things struck from the weekly grocery list. I went back to the way of cooking I was taught by my mother and grandmother.

"We Ate Well Enough"

When I wanted to make chicken soup, I started with a chicken. Add some rice and vegetables and you have a balanced, nutritious and filling meal.

Take some of the chicken meat, shred it in some barbecue sauce, add a side of potatoes, and you have another meal.

One chicken created two dinners, and enough leftovers from both for a couple lunches. True, it is much easier to open a can or pop a tray in the microwave, but those meals are nutritionally inferior as well as less tasty than food made from scratch. And much, much more expensive.

So, while there were no steaks in my house and we ate more canned and frozen vegetables than I prefer, we ate well enough.

What we didn't eat was fast food, or in any restaurants, for that matter. It simply was not in the budget. Do I want to go back to

How the Supplemental Nutrition Assistance Program (SNAP) Works

The following chart shows how food stamp money flows from the government to recipients to corporations. Some argue that letting people spend food stamps on fast food just puts taxpayer dollars into corporate pockets.

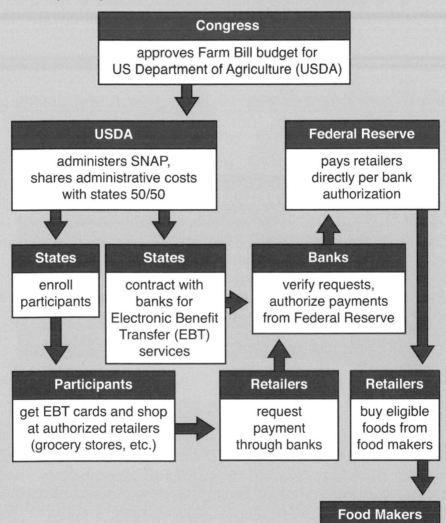

Congress
approves Farm Bill budget for US Department of Agriculture (USDA)

USDA
administers SNAP, shares administrative costs with states 50/50

Federal Reserve
pays retailers directly per bank authorization

States
enroll participants

States
contract with banks for Electronic Benefit Transfer (EBT) services

Banks
verify requests, authorize payments from Federal Reserve

Participants
get EBT cards and shop at authorized retailers (grocery stores, etc.)

Retailers
request payment through banks

Retailers
buy eligible foods from food makers

Food Makers

Taken from: US Government Accountability Office. "Food Stamp Program: Options for Delivering Financial Incentives to Participants for Purchasing Targeted Food," July 2008. Michelle Simon. Food Stamps: Follow the Money: Are Corporations Profiting from Hungry Americans?" Eat Drink Politics, June 2012.

peanut butter and jelly sandwiches in my son's lunch box every day? Was I happy not being able to take my son to the golden arches [McDonald's] when I didn't feel like cooking? Did I feel I had a right to these things? No, no and Hell No!

The Government Should Not Buy People Fast Food

We need to pay very careful attention to our elected officials on this issue, and woe to any local politician dumb enough or evil enough to support this initiative. We, the voters, your constituents, are tired of being insulted by your obvious low opinion of our collective intelligence.

Show me where ordering a No. 1 with cheese and a large Coke, paid for with tax dollars, is a constitutionally protected right. Until then, do not insult your constituents by supporting this latest instance of corporate malfeasance.

EVALUATING THE AUTHOR'S ARGUMENTS:

To make her argument that fast food need not be part of a low-budget diet, Denise Williams recounts a time in her life when she was on food stamps. Does her personal experience with this issue make you more or less likely to agree with her perspective on this issue? Explain your reasoning.

Facts About Fast Food

Editor's note: These facts can be used in reports to add credibility when making important points or claims.

Facts About Fast-Food Consumption

As reported by food journalist Eric Schlosser, author of *Fast Food Nation*:

- One-fourth of Americans consume fast food every day.
- The average American eats three hamburgers and four orders of French fries each week.

The US Department of Agriculture (USDA) contends that 30 percent of American children consume fast food on any given day.

According to *Understanding Childhood Obesity* [2011] by the American Heart Association (AHA):

- In the late 1970s American children ate 17 percent of their meals away from home, and fast food made up 2 percent of their diet.
- By the late 1990s children dined out for 30 percent of their meals, and fast food increased to 10 percent of their diet.
- From 1972 to 1995 the number of fast-food restaurants more than doubled.
- Poorer neighborhoods and areas with more minorities have fewer food markets, making fast-food restaurants the most accessible meal option for many families. In one study, wealthy areas had three times as many supermarkets as did low-income neighborhoods.

Facts About Fast Food and Health

According to the National Institutes of Health, one fast-food meal often contains as many calories as a person needs for an entire day.

A study published in the AHA's journal *Circulation* in 2012 compared adults who eat fast food to those who do not. They found:

- People who consume fast food at least twice a week are 27 percent more likely to develop diabetes.
- Those who eat fast food at least twice a week are at a 56 percent greater risk of dying from heart disease.
- When fast-food consumption increased to at least four times a week, people were almost 80 percent more likely to die of heart disease.

The 2010 report *Fast Food FACTS (Food Advertising to Children and Teens Score): Evaluating Fast Food Nutrition and Marketing to Youth*, published by Yale, examined meal options at fast food restaurants. It revealed that:

- Some fast-food side dishes contained fifteen hundred calories, as much as two meals' worth of calories.
- At all but two restaurants studied, dollar or value menu items geared toward people on a budget had significantly more calories and sodium than regular menu foods had.
- At fast-food restaurants that did provide nutritious food choices, these healthy items made up only 7 percent of their menu.
- Menu options designated as healthy were often high in sodium.

Facts About Fast Food and Kids

According to the Centers for Disease Control and Prevention's National Center for Health Statistics, obesity among American children aged six to nineteen rose from about 5 percent in the early 1970s to 16 percent in 2002, while the number of fast-food restaurants doubled in the same period.

A 2009 study sponsored by the Robert Wood Johnson Foundation asserts that teenagers who bring meals from home to school every day:

- eat fast food and drink soda less often than those who do not bring their lunch to school.

- eat nearly five servings more of fruits and vegetables per week.

According to *The Effect of Fast Food Restaurants on Obesity*, published by the National Bureau of Economic Research in 2009:

- 65 percent of high schools in California are within a half mile of a fast-food restaurant.
- High school freshmen are 5.2 percent more likely to be obese if there is a fast-food establishment within a tenth of a mile of their school.
- High schools located near fast-food restaurants tend to have heavier students, while being close to other types of restaurants has no effect on students' weight.
- Schools within a tenth of a mile of a fast-food restaurant tend to have slightly more low-income students, more Hispanic students, lower test scores, and are more likely to be in poorer areas.

Facts About Fast-Food Marketing
According to Yale's Rudd Center for Food Policy and Obesity:

- Fast-food companies spend about $4.2 billion a year on advertising.
- Young people saw more than one thousand television ads for fast-food restaurants in 2009.
- In 2012 Coca Cola and McDonald's sponsored the Summer Olympic Games; this sponsorship included toys and campaigns aimed at children.
- Mobile app games designed for kids often feature fast foods like ice cream, corn dogs, French fries, and hamburgers. Some of the apps are sponsored by food companies.
- In the United States in 2009 the average preschooler viewed 2.8 commercials for fast-food restaurants every day; the average child saw 3.5 fast-food ads each day; and the average teenager saw 4.7 fast-food ads per day.
- More than 13 percent of parents said that they bought a kids' meal at McDonald's or Burger King because their child wanted the toy.

The Food and Drug Administration spends $2 million a year to educate Americans about the health consequences of eating fast food.

The book *Fast Food Nation* reports that 96 percent of American schoolchildren can identify Ronald McDonald. Only Santa Claus was more recognized.

Facts About Fast-Food Regulations

According to a 2010 study review led by the director of the Center for Health and Public Policy Studies, common suggestions to limit Americans' consumption of fast foods include:

- Require food companies to identify ingredients and post warnings
- Bring lawsuits against food manufacturers for false advertising and failing to disclose health risks
- Regulate marketing of foods to children
- Tax high-sugar foods that lack nutrients, like soda
- Limit the amount of sodium allowed in restaurant foods
- Conduct media campaigns to educate people about sodium content in prepared foods
- Pass zoning laws to limit the location of fast-food restaurants
- Ban specific ingredients deemed to be unhealthy, such as trans-fats

In 2010 President Barack Obama signed a law requiring fast-food chain restaurants to:

- Provide calorie counts for food items on menus and menu boards
- Print on the menu the daily recommended number of calories that people should consume
- Offer written nutritional information including the calories in each food item; the number of calories from fat; and each serving's amount of total fat, saturated fat, cholesterol, sodium, carbohydrates, sugar, dietary fiber, and protein

Organizations to Contact

The editors have compiled the following list of organizations concerned with the issues debated in this book. The descriptions are derived from materials provided by the organizations. All have publications or information available for interested readers. The list was compiled on the date of publication of the present volume; the information provided here may change. Be aware that many organizations take several weeks or longer to respond to inquiries, so allow as much time as possible for the receipt of requested materials.

American Diabetes Association (ADA)
1701 N. Beauregard St.
Alexandria, VA 22311
(800) 342-2383
e-mail: askADA@diabetes.org
website: www.diabetes.org

The ADA, a not-for-profit health advocacy organization, works to prevent and cure diabetes, an obesity-related disease. Since food and good nutrition are critical to managing diabetes, the ADA educates people about lifestyle changes and disease prevention. As a part of its program, the ADA provides a guide to eating out and tips for how to order healthier items while dining at restaurants and fast-food establishments.

American Obesity Association (AOA)
8757 Georgia Ave., Ste. 1320
Silver Spring, MD 20910
(301) 563-6526
website: www.obesity.org

The AOA is the leading scientific organization dedicated to the study of obesity and its health effects. Its researchers seek to understand the causes and treatment of obesity while also keeping the medical community informed of the latest advances in research. It publishes the journal *Obesity*, and several newsletters and reports found on its website discuss the effects of fast food on obesity.

Center for Science in the Public Interest (CSPI)
1220 L St. NW, Ste. 300
Washington, DC 20005
(202) 332-9110
e-mail: cspi@cspinet.org
website: www.cspinet.org

Formed in 1971, the CSPI is a nonprofit education and consumer advocacy organization dedicated to fighting for government food policies and corporate practices that promote healthy diets. The CSPI also works to prevent deceptive marketing practices and ensures that science is used for public welfare. It publishes *Nutrition Action Healthletter*, the most widely circulated health newsletter in North America. Several of its publications are critical of fast-food marketing and nutritional content, and the group is a supporter of restaurant labeling laws.

Food Marketing Institute (FMI)
2345 Crystal Dr., Ste. 800
Arlington, VA 22202
(202) 452-8444
website: www.fmi.org

The FMI conducts programs in public affairs, food safety, research, education, and industry relations on behalf of food retailers and wholesalers in the United States and around the globe. The Health and Wellness section on its website provides information about nutrition, nutrition labeling, and obesity.

Food Research and Action Center (FRAC)
1875 Connecticut Ave. NW, Ste. 540
Washington, DC 20009
(202) 986-2200
website: www.frac.org

FRAC is the leading national nonprofit organization working to improve public policies and public-private partnerships to eradicate hunger and poor nutrition in the United States. FRAC serves as a watchdog of regulations and policies affecting the poor. It conducts public information campaigns, including the Campaign to End Childhood Hunger, to ensure that children of low-income families receive healthy and nutritious food so that they are able to learn and grow.

National Council of Chain Restaurants (NCCR)
325 Seventh St. NW, Ste. 1100
Washington, DC 20004
(202) 626-8189
e-mail: grannisk@nrf.com
website: www.nccr.net

The NCCR is the national trade association representing the chain restaurant industry and its 125,000 facilities. The NCCR works to advance sound public policy that best serves the interests of chain restaurants and the 3 million people they employ. Its website provides up-to-date industry news, links to a number of government-relations resources, a Legislative Action Center where viewers can research legislation and learn how to work with Congress, and for members of the site, access to *NCCR Highlights Newsletter*.

National Restaurant Association
1200 Seventeenth St. NW
Washington, DC 20036
(202) 331-5900
e-mail: webchef@restaurant.org
website: www.restaurant.org

The National Restaurant Association represents, educates, and promotes America's $566 billion restaurant business. It promotes a pro-restaurants agenda, argues on behalf of the restaurant industry before Congress and federal regulatory agencies, and works to battle anti-restaurant initiatives. Reports, publications, press releases, and research about important topics affecting the food industry can all be found on its website, including the *2009 Restaurant Industry Forecast*.

Rudd Center for Food Policy & Obesity
Yale University
309 Edwards St.
New Haven, CT 06511
website: www.yaleruddcenter.org

The Rudd Center is a nonprofit research and public policy organization devoted to improving the world's diet, preventing obesity, and reducing weight stigma. The center serves as a leading research institution and clearinghouse for resources that add to the understanding of the complex forces affecting how we eat, how we stigmatize overweight and obese people, and how we can change.

US Department of Agriculture (USDA)
Food and Nutrition Service
1400 Independence Ave. SW
Washington, DC 20250
(202) 720-2791
website: www.usda.gov

The Food and Nutrition Service is an agency of the USDA that is responsible for administering the nation's domestic nutrition assistance programs. It provides prepared meals, food assistance, and nutrition education materials to one in five Americans. The agency also encourages children and teens to follow the healthy eating guidelines set by MyPyramid in its "Eat Smart, Play Hard" campaign.

US Food and Drug Administration (FDA)
5600 Fishers Ln.
Rockville, MD 20857
(888) 463-6332
e-mail: webmail@oc.fda.gov
website: www.fda.gov

The FDA is a public health agency charged with protecting American consumers by enforcing the Federal Food, Drug, and Cosmetic Act and several related public health laws. The FDA sends investigators and inspectors into the field to ensure that the country's almost ninety-five thousand FDA-regulated businesses are compliant. Its publications include government documents, reports, fact sheets, and press announcements. It also provides food-labeling guidance and regulatory information for restaurants on its website.

For Further Reading

Books

Cardello, Hank, and Doug Garr. *Stuffed: An Insider's Look at Who's (Really) Making America Fat and How the Food Industry Can Fix It.* New York: Ecco, 2010. Argues that the obesity epidemic is connected to food businesses that control almost everything the average American eats.

Food, Inc.: A Participant Guide: How Industrial Food Is Making Us Sicker, Fatter, and Poorer—And What You Can Do About It. New York: PublicAffairs, 2009. A companion book to the popular documentary *Food, Inc.,* this collection of essays examines and challenges the corporate food industry.

Johansen, Lisa Tillinger. *Fast Food Vindication.* Stevenson Ranch, CA: J Murray, 2012. This dietitian argues that the fast-food industry is actually a positive force in society, arguing that it provides a product that meets high standards of quality and safety, often healthier than meals served at home and in sit-down restaurants.

Ladner, Peter. *The Urban Food Revolution: Changing the Way We Feed Cities.* Gabriola Island, BC: New Society, 2011. Offers recommendations for community food security.

Nestle, Marion. *Food Politics: How the Food Industry Influences Nutrition, and Health.* Berkeley: University of California Press, 2007. This widely celebrated book explores how the food industry—through lobbying, advertising, and the co-opting of experts—influences our dietary choices to our detriment.

Winne, Mark. *Closing the Food Gap: Resetting the Table in the Land of Plenty.* Boston: Beacon, 2009. Written by a food activist and journalist, this book explores how America's food gap (between those of high and low income levels) has widened since the 1960s and examines the paradox of how the demand for fresh food is rising in one population as fast as rates of obesity and diabetes are rising in another.

Periodicals and Internet Sources

American Academy of Pediatrics. "Children, Adolescents, Obesity, and the Media," *Pediatrics,* June 27, 2011, vol. 128, no. 1, pp. 201–208. http://pediatrics.aappublications.org/content/128/l/201.full.html.

Basu, Rituparna. "Ever-More Government Control in Fast Food," *The A&T Register (Greensboro, NC),* November 3, 2010. www.ncatregister.com/theword/op_ed/ever-more-government-control-in-fast-food/article_3cea96c3-bc4e-5b7d-9238-22e5de45cb26.html.

Berger, Eric. "To Be Effective, Scientists Say Junk Food Taxes Must Be Very High," *Houston Chronicle,* May 18, 2012. http://blog.chron.com/sciguy/2012/05/to-be-effective-scientists-say-junk-food-taxes-must-be-very-high/.

Bittman, Mark. "Is Junk Food Really Cheaper?," *New York Times,* September 24, 2011. www.nytimes.com/2011/09/25/opinion/sunday/is-junk-food-really-cheaper.html?pagewanted=all.

Briggs, Bill. "Fast-Food Giants Try to Cut the 'Guilty,' Leave the 'Pleasure,'" NBCnews.com, August 21, 2012. http://bottomline.nbcnews.com/news/2012/08/21/13300292-fast-food-giants-try-to-cut-the-guilty-leave-the-pleasure?lite.

Bruegel, Martin. "The 'Science' of Calorie Information," *New York Times,* September 19, 2012. www.nytimes.com/2012/09/19/opinion/the-science-of-calorie-information.html.

Center for Science in the Public Interest. "Nutrition Labeling at Fast-Food and Other Chain Restaurants," Phila.gov. www.phila.gov/health/pdfs/WhyMenu.pdf.

Cummins, Ronnie. "Should Congress Enact Taxes on Obesity-Producing Foods? Yes," *Denver Post,* May 13, 2012. www.denverpost.com/opinion/ci_20596960/should-congress-enact-taxes-obesity-producing-foods.

Currie, Janet, Stefano DellaVigna, Enrico Moretti, and Vikran Pathania. "The Effect of Fast Food Restaurants on Obesity," American Association of Wine Economics, AAWE Working Paper no. 33, February 2009. www.wine-economics.org/workingpapers/AAWE_WP33.pdf.

Dailey, Kate. "Will Soda Taxes and Fast-Food Bans Fix Obesity?," *The Daily Beast,* November 16, 2010. www.thedailybeast.com /newsweek/2010/ll/16/will-soda-taxes-and-fast-food-bans-fix -obesity.html.

Davis, Brennan, and Christopher Carpenter. "Proximity of Fast Food Restaurants to School and Adolescent Obesity," *American Journal of Public Health,* March 2009, vol. 99, no. 3, pp. 505–510. www .foodpolitics.com/wp-content/uploads/fast-food.pdf.

Drum, Kevin. "Food Deserts Not to Blame for Obesity and Poor Nutrition," *Mother Jones,* April 20, 2012. www.motherjones.com /kevin-drum/2012/04/food-deserts-obesity-nutrition.

Fisman, Ray. "Don't Ban Big Gulps," Slate.com, September 11, 2012. www.slate.com/articles/business/the_dismal_science /2012/09/bloombergs_soda_ban_taxing_sugary_beverages_is_a _better_more_effective_idea_.single.html.

Gadsden Times. "Fast Food Stamps?," September 8, 2011. www.gads dentimes.com/article/20110908/NEWS/110909810?p=l&tc=pg.

Gearhardt, Ashley N., Carlos M. Grilo, Ralph J. DiLeone, Kelly D. Brownell, and Marc N. Potenza. "Can Food Be Addictive? Public Health and Policy Implications," *Addiction,* June 2011. www.yaleruddcenter.org/resources/upload/docs/what/addiction /AddictionPublicHealthandPolicyImplications_Addiction_6.1l.pdf.

Harlan, Tim. "Why Fast Food Isn't Cheaper than Healthy Food," *Huffington Post,* May 18, 2011. www.huffingtonpost.com/tim -harlan-md/health-food-prices_b_862770.html.

Harris, Kimi. "Disney's Junk Food Ban Doesn't Address Root Issues," *Forbes,* June 6, 2012. www.forbes.com/sites/eco-nomics /2012/06/06/op-ed-disneys-junk-food-ban-doesnt-address-root- issues/.

Hedgecock, Roger. "Happy Meal Toy Ban Backfires, the California Way," *Human Events,* December 1, 2011. www.humanevents .com/2011/12/01/happy-meal-toy-ban-backfires-the-california -way/.

Kolata, Gina. "Food Deserts and Obesity Role Challenged," *New York Times,* April 18, 2012. www.nytimes.com/2012/04/18/health

/research/pairing-of-food-deserts-and-obesity-challenged-in
-studies.html?_r=2.

Littlejohn, Richard. "Taxing Fast Food Won't Persuade People to
Eat Lentils and Mung Beans," *Daily Mail,* April 16, 2012. www
.dailymail.co.uk/debate/article-2130690/Taxing-fast-food-won-t
-persuade-people-eat-lentils-mung-beans.html.

Luciani, Patrick. "Tax Junk Science, Not Junk Food," *Huffington
Post,* May 18, 2012. www.huffingtonpost.ca/patrick-luciani
/junk-food-tax-canada_b_1524430.html.

Mangu-War, Katherine. "McDonald's to Kids: Apple Slices for All,
Whether or Not You Want Them," Reason.com, July 26, 2011.
http://reason.com/archives/2011/07/26/mcdonalds-to-kids-apple
-slices.

Martin, Roland. "Parents, Don't Blame Happy Meals," CNN.com,
December 17, 2010. http://articles.cnn.com/2010-12-17/opinion
/martin.happy.meals_1_parents-toys-trans-fats?_s=PM:OPINION.

Mulshine, Paul. "Don't Ban Soda, Tax It," New Jersey.com, June 3,
2012. http://blog.nj.com/njv_paul_mulshine/2012/06/soft_drinks
.html.

Nathanial, Jerome. "Obesity Food Deserts Have Given Way to
Food Swamps," PolicyMic, www.policymic.com/articles/7176
/obesity-food-deserts-have-given-way-to-food-swamps.

Park, Alice. "NYC's Trans Fat Ban Worked: Fast-Food Diners Are
Eating Healthier," *Time,* July 17, 2012. http://healthland.time
.com/2012/07/17/nycs-trans-fat-ban-worked-fast-food-diners-are
-eating-healthier/.

Philpott, Tom. "Is Cooking Really Cheaper than Fast Food?,"
Mother Jones, October 4, 2011. www.motherjones.com/tom-phil
pott/2011/10/cooking-really-cheaper-junk-food-mark-bittman.

Saletan, William. "Food Apartheid: Banning Fast Food in Poor
Neighborhoods," Slate.com, July 31, 2008. www.slate.com/id/21
96397/.

Sirico, Robert A. "Hate the Sin, Tax the Sinner?," *The American
Magazine,* May 20, 2009. www.american.com/archive/2009/may
-2009/hate-the-sin-tax-the-sinner.

Soupcoff, Marni. "Food Apartheid," *Regulation,* Fall 2008, p. 60. www.cato.org/pubs/regulation/regv31n3/v31n3-final.pdf.

Stier, Jeff. "The Happy Meal Ban Flops," *National Review,* December 1, 2011. www.nationalreview.com/articles/284509/happy-meal -ban-flops-jeff-stier?pg=l.

Waugh, Rob. "Adverts for Fast Food Make Children Fat," *Daily Mail,* April 30, 2012. www.dailymail.co.uk/sciencetech/article -2137186/Adverts-fast-food-make-children-fat-Kids-recognise chicken-hamburger-TWICE-likely-obese.html.

Wirthman, Lisa. "Should Food Stamps Be Used for Fast Food?," *Denver Post,* November 16, 2011. www.denverpost.com/perspective /ci_19233373.

Websites

Center for Science in the Public Interest: Menu Labeling (www .menulabeling.org). Examines menu labeling, including links to fact sheets, descriptions of legislation, videos, and a restaurant quiz to test knowledge of the nutrition information of common menu items.

Centers for Disease Control and Prevention: A Look Inside Food Deserts (www.cdc.gov/features/fooddeserts/). An in-depth look at food deserts—geographic areas that lack access to stores that sell affordable fresh produce and other healthful foods—including over-views, reports, nutrition resources, and a section entitled "How to Tell If You Live in a Food Desert."

Slow Food (www.slowfood.com). Explores the slow-food philosophy, which advocates for fresh, healthful, seasonal, locally grown food that does not harm the environment, animal welfare, or human health.

Index

Picture Credits